#HipHopEd: The Compilation on Hip-hop Education

Revolutionizing Urban Education: Hip-hop, Pedagogy, and Communities

VOLUME 1

Scope

This series consists of books written for all stakeholders in education including undergraduate and graduate students of education, teachers, parents, and the community at large. The volumes bridge research, theory, personal anecdotes and practice, and interrogates and provides recommendations for schools and communities, specifically in urban spaces. Books in this series focus on utilizing hip-hop as education to transform urban education and schools, and to introduce critical pedagogical ways to engage communities, and schools. Educators, students, community members, and academics are given opportunities to understand the essential nature of voice and activism. This work is necessary to transform schools and communities to better represent the young people they were built to serve.

The titles published in this series are listed at *brill.com/hhed*

#HipHopEd: The Compilation on Hip-hop Education

Volume 1: Hip-hop as Education, Philosophy, and Practice

Edited by

Christopher Emdin and Edmund Adjapong

BRILL

SENSE

LEIDEN | BOSTON

All chapters in this book have undergone peer review.

Library of Congress Cataloging-in-Publication Data is available online at http://catalog.loc.gov

Typeface for the Latin, Greek, and Cyrillic scripts: "Brill". See and download: brill.com/brill-typeface.

ISSN 2589-5796
ISBN 978-90-04-37185-9 (paperback)
ISBN 978-90-04-37186-6 (hardback)
ISBN 978-90-04-37187-3 (e-book)

This book is printed on acid-free paper and produced in a sustainable manner.

To the late great Joe Kincheloe

Contents

Foreword: Bringin' It

Shirley R. Steinberg
@Youthcultureca

As the first volume in the new series, *Revolutionizing Urban Education: Hip-hop, Pedagogy, and Communities,* the authors in Christopher Emdin's and Edmund Adjapong's book stand in a cypher interlaced through hip-hop, social justice, education, and society. *#HipHopEd: The Compilation on Hip-hop Education* is the anchor book in the first set of reference books which will serve to define and redefine not only education, but hip-hop itself. Hip-hop selves often left at the door of schools are empowered to retrieve themselves in a co-generative approach to naming a pedagogy which is philosophical, cultural, socially just, and natural. Unifying ways of knowing through the culture of hip-hop, this book puts forward the alternative to what Donaldo Macedo refers to as the stupidification of education.

Make no mistake, #HipHopEd is not just a funky way to engage kids, employing it does not mean being *that cool teacher* who lets the kids listen to music, dance, and chill. Educating with hip-hop demands that the teacher knows the curriculum, the subject, the topic *and* is an expert on the history, social significance, and praxis of hip-hop. Bringing one's authentic self is crucial to #HipHopEd. Understanding that the hip-hop is a global culture, not a subculture, and the significance of its contextualization to children and youth is essential. #HipHopEd requires rigor, commitment, engagement, and knowledge; it is a social responsibility for activist teachers to acknowledge that education must be for the whole.

Understanding and identifying sources of power is central to hip-hop. Rooted in a critical theoretical notion that enlightenment emerges when power is named and revealed, hip-hop's seeds were sown from the beats and words heard and echoed on the streets of the marginalized. Challenges to social and political structures grew from the rhymes, promise and regeneration became the roots for a culture. The ability to pinpoint power reveals that humans are "acculturated and schooled to feel comfortable in relations of either domination or subordination rather than equality and interdependence" (Steinberg, 2010), early hip-hop was instrumental in bringing this revelation to those who suffered the oppressions of poverty and racism. Grandmaster Flash and the Furious Five (1982) uncovered and blasted an eyes-closed society which pushed Black men to the edge in a society set up to fail, to ghettoize and to drown. Instead of a traditional blues lamentation of being *done wrong*, "The Message" was laid down to accentuate a pushback noting the institutionalized and governmentalized despondency Black men often felt. By naming power in this way, society is called out, not the oppressed. Naming power is a two-fold act in an emancipatory identity: Paulo Freire taught that those who are oppressed continue that oppression until they are able to (1) realize and (2) identify the source. When that identity is made, the pedagogical change facilitates empowerment.

As the first incarnation of our new series, *Revolutionizing Urban Education,* Chris, Edmund, and authors have invited us to embody #HipHopEd as a critical pedagogical endeavor, an aesthetically-inspired curriculum, and a gathering of unshackled ways of knowing. By entering this cypher, readers will entwine their own beats, words, and moves...creating and re-creating ourselves as community.

References

Bootee, D. (1982). The message. On *Grandmaster flash and the furious five* [Recorded]. Englewood, NJ: Sugar Hill.

Steinberg, S. R. (2010). Power, emancipation, and complexity: Employing critical theory. *Power and Education, 2*(2), 140–141.

Acknowledgements

For my brothers Timothy David Jones and Amil Cook. Thank you for your devotion to the work. To Ian Levy for the mental health section edits and all around dopeness. To Malcolm, Sydney and Eb. Clique!!!!
– *Christopher Emdin*

For hip-hop. If it were not for you, I wouldn't be here. To Sara and the Adjapong family, thank you for all of your guidance and support.
– *Edmund Adjapong*

Notes on Contributors

Edmund Adjapong

is an assistant professor of Educational Studies at Seton Hall University and a faculty fellow at the Institute of Urban and Minority Education. He is also the director of the Science Genius Program and Science Genius Academy. Dr. Adjapong has published his research on Hip-hop Education and equity in STEM (Science, Technology, Engineering, and Mathematics) in many journals such as the *Journal for Urban Learning, Teaching and Research* and the *Journal of Critical Education.*

Joshua Childs

is an assistant professor of Educational Policy and Planning in the Department of Educational Administration. Joshua received his PhD in Learning Sciences and Policy at the University of Pittsburgh. Joshua's research focuses on the role of interorganizational networks, cross-sector collaborations, and strategic alliances to address complex educational issues. Specifically, his work examines collaborative approaches involving community organizations and stakeholders that have the potential to improve academic achievement and reduce opportunity gaps for students in urban and rural schools. Joshua is an RGK Faculty Fellow and a faculty fellow with the Institute for Urban Policy Research & Analysis.

Francesca D'Amico-Cuthbert

is the author of *Welcome to the Terrordome: Contesting the Duppy State and the Discourses of the Dispossessed through American Rap Music, 1979–1995,* which examines how rappers use culture as a space of strategic contestation in order to contend with the concerns of a Black public sphere, while also provoking questions and initiating debates over race and power in America. Her work attempts to rethink how rappers used culture to nurture potentially subversive forms of interiority, render public the private geographies of Blackness, and ultimately determine which issues moved from the margins to the broader national stage – effectively casting culture as relevant to political discourse. Francesca has developed and implemented a curriculum intended for elementary and high school students that approaches the Ontario (Canada) core curriculum subjects of history/social studies, math, science and language through the history and tools of hip-hop culture.

Christopher Emdin

is an Associate Professor in the Department of Mathematics, Science and Technology at Teachers College, Columbia University; where he also serves as Director of Science Education at the Center for Health Equity and Urban Science Education. He is the author of the New York Times Bestseller *For White Folks Who Teach in the Hood ... and the Rest of Y'all Too: Reality Pedagogy and Urban Education* (Beacon, 2016), *Between the World and the Urban Classroom* (Sense, 2017) and *Urban Science Education for the Hip-hop Generation* (Sense, 2010).

Elicia Estime

is a student at the University of Rochester. She is an artist and poet originally from Miami, Florida. Elicia is passionate about music and has performed at venues such as The Bitter End, The Freedman's Home, and many open mics all around NYC.

Jeremy Heyman

is a former chemist-turned-urban science educator whose passion evolved from solving structures of new molecules to exploring ways to engage more students in the STEM pipeline, and ultimately to expanding college access and success in among urban immigrant students. He was a founding science teacher at ELLIS; a public school in the Bronx serving 16–21 year-old newcomer immigrant ELLs. His roles over the years have ranged from teacher to college access and success counselor, STEM outreach coordinator, college readiness grant administrator, partnership-builder, and data specialist. He completed a PhD in Science Education at Columbia in 2016, focusing on access and persistence in STEM majors among ELL students from underserved high schools.

Kai Jones

is an English Educator at public school in the Bronx, NY. She graduated with a bachelors in English from Norfolk State University. During her tenure as an English teacher, she earned a master's degree from Lehman College in English Education and Educational Administration from Lamar University. She is currently doctoral student in Literacy at St. John's University. Kai enjoys writing and creating exciting, innovative classroom curricula.

Lauren Leigh Kelly

is an Assistant Professor of Urban Teacher Education at Rutgers University's Graduate School of Education. She is also the founder of the annual Hip-hop Youth Summit. Kelly taught high school English for ten years in New York where she also developed courses in Hip-hop Literature and Culture, Spoken Word poetry, and Theatre Arts. Kelly's research focuses on adolescent critical literacy development, Black feminist theory, critical consciousness, and critical hip-hop pedagogies. Kelly received her bachelor's degree in English from Wesleyan University; her master's in Adolescent Education from St. John's University; and her Ph.D. in English Education from Teachers College, Columbia University. Kelly's work on critical hip-hop literacies has been published in academic journals such as *Journal of Adolescent and Adult Literacy* and *English Journal*, and has been featured in *Education Week, Education Update,* and *School Library Journal.*

Tina Khan

is a math and science educator and has worked for the Toronto District School Board for the past 20 years. She holds a Master Degree in Education from the University of Toronto. Tina is the co-founder of the Each1 Teach1 Partnership, an innovative program to engage and empower Black youth in Toronto secondary schools. The mission of the program is to work with Black community artists and activists to teach themes of identity, culture, resistance and resilience. Tina organizes the Toronto District School Board's Hip-hop STEMposium conference, which focuses on introducing hip-hop pedagogy to educators in Toronto.

Gloria Ladson-Billings

is Professor Emerita and Kellner Family Chair of Urban Education in the Department of Curriculum & Instruction, Educational Policy Studies, Educational Leadership & Policy Analysis, and Afro-American Studies at the University of Wisconsin-Madison. She was the 2005–2006 President of the American Educational Research Association and is current president of the National Academy of Education.

Ian P. Levy

is a professor of school counseling at the University of Massachusetts-Boston. Ian's research interests include the examination of mental health practices in urban schools, including interrogating the role of the school counselor to ensure the emotional lives of young people are adequately addressed. Dr. Levy piloted the development, implementation, and evaluation of a hip-hop based counseling framework in urban schools. This program was featured on news outlets including the New York Times and CNN. In 2016, he was named the New York State School Counselor of the Year. Dr. Levy focuses on addressing the multifaceted roles of the school counselor. In 2017, he was named an emerging leader by the Association of Humanistic Counseling.

Bettina L. Love

is an award-winning author and Associate Professor of Educational Theory & Practice at the University of Georgia. Her research focuses on the ways in which urban youth negotiate hip-hop music and culture to form social, cultural, and political identities to create new and sustaining ways of thinking about urban education and intersectional social justice. Her research also focuses on how teachers and schools working with parents and communities can build communal, civically engaged, anti-racist, anti-homophobic, and anti-sexist educational, equitable classrooms. For her work in the field, in 2016, Dr. Love was named the Nasir Jones Hip-hop Fellow at the Hutchins Center for African and African American Research at Harvard University. In 2014, she was invited to the White House Research Conference on Girls to discuss her work focused on the lives of Black girls. In addition, she is the inaugural recipient of the Michael F. Adams award (2014) from the University of Georgia. She has also provided commentary for various news outlets including NPR, *The Guardian*, and the *Atlanta Journal Constitution*.

Matthew R. Morris

is an elementary educator, writer and anti-racism advocate in Toronto. He has written and spoken about teaching, race, and education. His work has been featured in the *Toronto Star, Huffington Post, Education Canada,* and *ETFO Voice Magazine.* He has spoken on the topics of equity, racism within schooling, new teacher preparation, and the cultural politics of education at various school boards and universities within Ontario. His TEDx talk, "The Fresh Prince syndrome," is a call to high schools to become more lax with their implicit curriculum if they want to reach many of the young black males that the system currently fails. He has worked for the Toronto District School Board for the past seven years and currently teaches middle school in inner city Toronto. He also has an M.A in Education from the Ontario Institute for Studies in Education (OISE) at the University of Toronto.

Cassandra Ogbevire

is a native of Chicago, Illinois who has dedicated her career to scholarship, advocacy, and education to ensure the holistic development of Black male adolescents. She's a graduate of Spelman College and a masters student at the Graduate School of Education at the University Pennsylvania in May 2018. Currently, Cassandra is a secondary ELA teacher at the Boys' Latin Charter School of Philadelphia.

Courtney Rose

is a doctoral candidate in the Curriculum & Teaching Ed.D. program, with a concentration in Curriculum Studies at Teachers College, Columbia University. She also holds an M.Ed. from the Harvard Graduate School of Education in Human Development & Psychology and a B.A. in Elementary Education from the University of Florida. Prior to joining the TC community, Courtney taught upper elementary school Math & Science for three years in the Jacksonville Public School System (Jacksonville, FL). Currently, her research interests include the development and implementation of social justice-oriented critical and culturally relevant instructional practices and curricular designs. Specifically, she focuses on the development and preparation of pre- and in-service teachers to enact such practices in K-12 educational settings.

Shirley R. Steinberg

is Research Professor of Critical Youth Studies at the University of Calgary. An urban educator, she holds research appointments in Spain and the UK, where she collaborates in community education and youth activism. Her work centers on critical pedagogy, social justice, diversity, and critical media literacy. With Priya Parmar and Shirley pioneered the *Lyrically Minded* program in Brooklyn schools in the 90s, bringing hip-hop teaching artists into English classes. Her new book is *Activists Under 30: Youth as Agents of Social Change*. With Christopher Emdin and Edmund Adjapong, she is the co-editor of the new series, *Revolutionizing Urban Education: Hip-hop, Pedagogy, and Communities*. Shoutout to Winthrop Holder from Walton High School, The Bronx, who took her into the *One Mic* fold and shared his precious students.

Raphael Travis

engages in research, practice and consultancy work that emphasizes positive youth development over the life-course, resilience, and civic engagement. He also investigates creative arts, especially Hip-hop culture, as a source of health and well-being in people's lives. Dr. Travis is an Associate Professor and BSW Program Director at Texas State University in the School of Social Work. Dr. Travis' latest research appears in a variety of academic journals and he is the author of the book *The Healing Power of Hip Hop*. He had three goals for the book: to help people understand how hip-hop improves lives and communities; to introduce a new generation of "cultural ambassadors" or leaders who understand how hip-hop culture can be used positively; and to celebrate opportunities available from our awareness. Dr. Raphael Travis Jr., LCSW, holds degrees from University of Virginia, University of Michigan, and University of California at Los Angeles.

Tara Ware

is a science educator and teacher leader who has taught at Validus Preparatory Academy, a public school, in the Bronx for over 10 years. Tara has been participating teacher in the Science Genius B.A.T.T.L.E.S. program since its inception because she understands the influence that music, culture and performance has on students' engagement and understanding of rigorous science content.

Melvin L. Williams

is an assistant professor of communication studies at Pace University, where he teaches undergraduate courses in critical media studies, popular culture, and race and ethnicity in the media. A native of Memphis, Tennessee, Dr. Williams earned his Ph.D. in Communication, Culture, and Media Studies and a graduate certificate in Women's Studies from Howard University, as well as his Bachelor and Master's degrees from Tennessee State University. As a communication scholar and celebrated culturist, he examines the intersections of race, gender, and sexuality in popular culture. Specifically, his research considers the political ramifications of popular culture to investigate how minority communities use its mediums to address disparaging media representations. Dr. Williams has published research in several books and journals, including *Feminist Theory and Pop Culture, The Journal on Race, Gender, and Class, Spectrum,* and most recently, *The Journal of Hip Hop Studies.*

Introduction

Christopher Emdin

#HipHopEd is a sociopolitical movement that utilizes both online and offline platforms to advance the utility of hip-hop as a theoretical framework and practical approach to teaching and learning. The movement is aimed at disrupting the oppressive structures of schools and schooling for marginalized youth through a reframing of hip-hop in the public sphere. We accomplish this goal by bringing students, parents, teachers, and community members together to work towards the advancement of the educative dimensions of the hip-hop culture. #HipHopEd's academic roots include, but are not limited to the fields of education, sociology, anthropology and cultural studies. Participants in the movement draw their most distinct academic connections to the field of hip-hop studies; which in many ways, is the stem from which this branch of study has grown and established itself.

The brilliant work of scholars like Imani Perry, Tricia Rose, Michael Eric Dyson, Mark Anthony Neal, Murray Forman, Bajarti Kitawana, S. Craig Watkins, and Jeff Chang provided a space for the critical study of hip-hop in academia. These authors, and the many more scholars who brought hip-hop into fields like African American studies, philosophy, and English, provided in depth studies of a wide range of topics that range from feminism to race and racism. However, much of their work only tangentially engaged in and with education. The few that did, troubled/explored hip-hop in higher education with little to no focus on pedagogy or K-12 educational spaces. In response, #HipHopEd is explicit about its focus on the science and art of teaching and learning. We argue that hip-hop embodies the awareness, creativity and innovation that are at the core of any true education. Our work brings visibility to the silenced narratives of academic achievement and love for education that exists among the hip-hop generation. We aim to showcase the brilliance, resilience, ingenuity and intellectual prowess of those who are embedded in hip-hop culture but may not have been successful in schools.

#HipHopEd acknowledges the need to reintroduce hip-hop to a generation of youth who have had their culture stolen, repackaged and sold back to them by the power wielders of the entertainment industry. We recognize the 3 P's of corporate hip-hop (purloin/package/profit) and the effect it has on socioeconomically deprived youth enveloped in a culture of capitalism. We see the ways that corporate hip-hop has led our artists to intentionally engage in and with content that does not reflect the culture in an attempt to sell and profit from images that have been constructed by media. We do not draw a line in the sand against artists that many of our youth admire and aspire to live like. Instead, we shed light on the ways that many artists have been shaped by an industry that stifles creativity and artistry by forcing young people to exist within very narrow parameters in order to be commercially successful. We see how this is correlated to the ways that hip-hop youth are shaped by schools to be less than who they are in order to be academically successful.

Hip-hop in its purest form thrives on synthesis and interdisciplinary, exposure and expansion, peace, unity, and having fun. It promotes creativity and freedom of expression. #HipHopEd does the same. We believe in no boundaries. We identify that there are aspects of formal education that are redeemable, but we fervently critique institutions that present themselves as our saviors. We never blindly accept their ways of knowing and being as a replacement for the hip-hop ways that we learn. At the same time, we recognize that engaging in #HipHopEd work requires entering in and owning academic spaces. In response, we focus on bringing the previously silenced and distorted voices of the hip-hop generation to the very institutions that inflicted the silencing and distorting while creating spaces for them to exist freely.

#HipHopEd highlights the flaws and hypocrisies in contemporary education from both within and outside of academia through a wide range of voices that have both been successful within and been pushed out of schools. We highlight the experiences of those who have been successful within schools but have not necessarily benefited from the enterprise, and those who have been pushed out who do not lack intelligence and/or academic capability. Furthermore, we work to bring the lip service paid to access/equity in education to the fore by highlighting the daily inequities those embedded in hip-hop experience both within and outside of schools and academia despite colorful equity laden mission statements and proclamations. #HipHopEd highlights and deconstructs the co-option of terms like social justice and cultural relevance by power wielders (district personnel, academics, government) and the ways that this negatively affects those invested in hip-hop who experience unjust pedagogies and distortions of their culture in schools on a daily basis.

In the last few years, many scholars have increasingly begun to engage in this work. Scholar practitioners like Gabriel Asheru Benn, Sam Seidel, Martha Diaz and academics like Bettina Love, Emery Petchauer, Ernest Morrell, Jeff Duncan Andrade, Samy Alim, Awad Ibrahim, Joycelyn Wilson and David Stovall have forged forward in making sense of how hip-hop and education come together. In a seminal book that brought together much of the work of the scholars named above, Hill (2009) coined the phrase Hip-hop Based Education (HHBE). In the text, Hill describes HHBE as an approach to using hip-hop text in transmitting disciplinary knowledge. In this work, and others that position their work as falling under the umbrella of HHBE, the focus is traditionally on literacy and English with a focus on the use of hip-hop lyrics/text to meet established academic standards. #HipHopEd(ucators) support this work, the assertions about the value of hip-hop lyrics and artists that undergird it, and the notion that hip-hop can be used to learn academic content. However, we push beyond having institutions just valuing hip-hop text, and towards a more radical position that does not seek permission and/or validation from schools. We argue that much of the existing work in hip-hop and education still functions within a paradigm that is rooted in a desire for acceptance from those outside of the culture. We ask why the beauty, complexity and brilliance of hip-hop lyrics has to be accepted by the same people and institutions that failed the young people who wrote them? Why must our work be limited to English classrooms and the humanities when hip-hop is just as aligned to science and mathematics? We argue that hip-hop education writ large must takes on a larger #HipHopEd philosophy that believes in the unapologetic framing of hip-hop as education.

We don't need education to base or connect itself to us if that education does not fully reflect us. The field of education must begin to make sense of hip-hop sensibilities that include dress, talk, and self-expression. The core elements of emceeing, b-boying, dee-jaying and graffiti must be seen as academic subjects and hip-hop must be seen as the curriculum and the pedagogy. #HipHopEd argues not for a basing of what we do in formal education, but for a philosophical and conceptual understanding of hip-hop as education. I see this approach as a critical hip-hop pedagogy (CHHP) with a revolutionary philosophy. This is #HipHopEd.

#HipHopEd(ucators) begin with the fundamental premise that schools as they currently exist are much further away from true education that hip-hop is. We refuse to marry hip-hop to a corrupt system that will inevitably bring flawed versions of hip-hop into classrooms, and then blame hip-hop writ large for its own lack of effectiveness. We cannot base an education designed to fail us on hip-hop because hip-hop represents everything that contemporary education is not. Education itself needs to be redefined. This is why we move forward with the basic argument and fundamental understanding that hip-hop is education.

Once we fully understand the #HipHopEd's guiding theories described above, we can argue for the substitution of the present approach to education with one that fully reflects the complexities of hip-hop. The buildings can remain the same, the job titles can remain the same, but everything that happens within schools as it relates to the education of youth from the hip-hop generation and beyond must be change. We do not expect this substitution to be seamless, or for those who benefit from the structure as it currently exists to hand over their power and control without a fight. In fact, we must expect their resistance and be prepared for battle. #HipHopEd holds all that is necessary (intellectually and morally) to justify our position and argue for it unabashedly and tirelessly. We will fight in the court of public opinion, the halls of academia, and within the walls of classrooms until hip-hop is established within schools as the primary approach for the delivery of instruction. While we may have first asked for hip-hop's cohabitation with the established structure in some classrooms, we now want the schools to ourselves through #HipHopEd because we are tired of seeing our youth being emotionally and intellectually slaughtered in traditional schools.

1   #HipHopEd(ucators)

#HipHopEd(ucators) recognize that the language of social justice and cultural relevance has been brought into schools and used as a tool to pacify those who advocate for true equity. We work to establish social justice and cultural relevance focused teaching that has hip-hop music, art, and culture as its anchor because the expression of a hip-hop identity has become the reason for certain populations to be pushed to the margins within schools and in society. Not only do # HipHopEd(ucators) use hip-hop as a tool to move youth to the center of the discourse on teaching and learning, they also work towards developing their own hip-hop identity. They study the culture and find an entry point for themselves. They learn that developing a hip-hop sensibility (a certain engagement/awareness of some aspect of the culture) and identity is an asset that is just as valuable as knowing the academic content to be delivered. They recognize that the absence of a hip-hop sensibility, and an inability to develop an authentic hip-hop identity, positions the educator or any professional working within schools as grossly deficient and unprepared for fully engaging young people.

There is an inherent role reversal and reframing in who is seen as prepared, smart, effective, and capable when it comes to #HipHopEd. Many who schools see as successes, we see as failures. Many who have been pushed out of schools, we see as geniuses. We challenge the notion that the few from the hip-hop generation who have found success within traditional schools by sacrificing or hiding their hip-hop identity are truly successes. This is particularly the case for people of color who are held as exemplars of who Black youth should model themselves after despite their betrayal or purposeful erasure of their culture. We challenges the notion that people who have been "successful" in traditional formal education can speak for, and to the needs of the majority – those who have been silenced and crushed by schooling (particularly those who are hip-hop). Finally, to be a #HipHopEd(ucator) is to challenge what teacher education programs and professional development initiatives are doing if they are not in some way engaging in, with, or through hip-hop.

The #HipHopEd(ucartor) recognizes that the silencing of the voice and crushing of the spirit has become the chief function of contemporary schools. This is not hyperbole or conjecture. There are actual daily processes where the overpowering and drowning out of the voice of hip-hop youth by either punishing those who speak about their negative experiences in schools (until they learn to be silent about their oppression) or completely ignoring their cries for change in schools are commonplace. Prominent examples of this silencing are evident in instances that range from school suspensions for critiquing a teacher to the deliberate ignoring of popular hip-hop artists' commentary on education despite the multiple platforms (music, speeches, and social media) where they speak directly about the dysfunction they have either witnessed or experienced in schools. When White youth can protest freely about school shootings and garner media and political attention while Black youth from the hip-hop generation are shunned and silenced for being the visceral, and kinesthetic selves they are within hip-hop, something is wrong. They are not even allowed to be themselves – let alone speak about how the system is failing them.

The #HipHopEd(ucator) makes it a mission to reveal that the work of schools to actively silence and crush hip-hop or hop-hopness (expressions of hip-hop) works in partnership with co-conspirators like corporate media-record labels and news stations; which have made it their task to make hip-hop that has educational/academic value less visible while propelling misogynist and violent caricatures of hip-hop that are skillfully packaged through well promoted music and reality television to look and feel like the real thing. We recognize that this partnership between the school and the media functions to brainwash the public into believing that hip-hop is superficial, violent and anti-intellectual despite the fact that these images only reflect a thin slice of a much more complex and overwhelmingly positive and educative culture. We defend the culture. We support the culture. We admonish our young griots for their missteps, but we work to correct them before we send them out to be made into caricatures by media.

Revealing well hidden truths about schools and their role as training facilities for socioeconomically disadvantaged youth of color is our function. We recognize that for urban youth of color, the brand of pedagogy that is in place within their schools is one that accentuates an approach to teaching and learning that fosters docility and passivity. In these institutions schooling revolves around training for following instructions and subservience. The #HipHopEd(uducator) makes it public that blind enculturation is the chief task of schools for urban youth of color and reimagine out loud what schools would/could look and feel like if hip-hop was the chief tool that guides instruction. We reject any pedagogy whose aim is to indoctrinate youth into norms that do not serve their interests or reflect the cultural norms of their communities. Rather, we highlight the pedagogical practices that are inherent to hip-hop, and then provide evidence for how they have positively impacted youth. In this process, we highlight the ways that traditional schooling has convinced many who were raised in and by hip-hop to abandon or ignore the hip-hop within them.

Many of the authors in this compilation and who will read this book are the #HipHopEd(ucators) who have been quietly working to counter the silencing, crushing and brainwashing in schools. They have been providing platforms for youth to share their voices on what affects them, working to empower them through affirmations about their worth, expanding the discourse on hip-hop in schools, and using the same platforms that institutions that hold power take up, to provide a counter narrative to the ways they describe our youth and our culture. Unfortunately, for too long, our work has existed in silos with people who often work independently in geographically wide ranging yet disconnected spaces pushing an "underground" and relatively invisible body of work while fighting vigorously against powerful local and global structures aimed at stamping out their work. For these #HipHopEd(ucators) in "the trenches," the work then becomes too tiresome to bear as the physical boundaries and labor of the work make both the body and the mind vulnerable to physical, emotional, and psychological fatigue.

This fatigue can be countered through more powerful and connected work that requires comrades in the work to create strong networks that not only promote the collective movement to bring hip-hop into schools, but to push the theoretical and practical foundations of the work further and deeper than any one person/group can do alone. This meeting of comrades is not only necessary for pushing our #HipHopEd work further and deeper, but it is essential for the protection of the work from imposters who take on the language and surface practices of hip-hop while basing their work in flawed notions of the culture.

When the educator works in isolation in a school setting, the relationship between the pedagogue and the power structure proves to be too much to sustain truly powerful work. The relationship between the educator and the school – which is perceived to be mutually beneficial and between two factions that are on the same side shifts when it involves the lone soldier #HipHopEd(ucator). This relationship, over time, too often becomes one where the pedagogue permits practices that compromise the authenticity of the work in exchange for an opportunity to keep doing some version of the work. Many a compromise has been made that would not have been necessary if the work that was being done in isolation was part of a larger initiative/network/consortium like the #HipHopEd chat that has both scholarly merit and practical impact.

2   The #HipHopEd Chat – Timothy David Jones

There are 168 hours in a week and for one of these hours, every week since November 16, 2010, a growing group of hip-hop stakeholders, fans and people who are curious about hip-hop and or education from all over the country (and now the world) take to Twitter to build, share and distribute knowledge using the hashtag #HipHopEd. During the 167 hours between the end of one week's chat and the start of next, the team and I deliberate over topics that are developed within the camp and/or suggested by members of our growing #HipHopEd community. Our brother Amil Cook (@amilcook) is responsible for capturing the subject matter of the weekly chat in a visual/flyer that arrives without fail every Tuesday morning. Once the flyer is done, we spend between 60 and 90 minutes promoting the chat via individual tweets to previous participants, and the rest of the magic happens on its own as retweets of the flyer are cycled across Twitter throughout the day as the community prepares for the cyber cypher – which starts at 9:00 pm EST.

We call our chat a "cyber cypher" because it is structured like a hip-hop cypher – where participants form a circle and exchange with each other fluidly. Many Twitter chats are structured to mimic panel discussions where there is a featured expert discussing a topic or responding to questions. The #HipHopEd chat is more like a gathering of MCs – where energy is generated by one individual, and then picked up by another with a goal of keeping the energy going. We perfected this model by doing – rather than by studying an existing model, and have allowed thousands of people to become as central to our exchanges as any of the founders of the chat. In the midst of tweets from the moderators and the regulars, one can always find a new person who we celebrate and make welcome. We strive to create a space where academic credentials don't matter, and value to the community is based solely on participation and the way what is shared is valued by the entire community. It is a beautiful thing when parents, Ph.D's, pupils, professionals, practitioners, and pioneers of hip-hop can come together in a space where a respect for hip-hop is the link that holds us all together. From different parts of the world, we hold the same mission of transforming education through hip-hop and support each other in our local endeavors as we construct a global movement. Concurrently, we have learned through Twitter about communicating our ideas in a way that gives the most impact given the structures of the online platform.

Over the years, we have created a formula of sorts for the most effective #HipHopEd tweets. This formula came from the challenges that participants had conveying thoughts they had held inside for years without a platform for sharing it. The more people participated in the #HipHopEd chat, and the more the core team started working together to ensure that all participants could have their voices heard, the more we came to understand how to share our insights about teaching and learning, and build capacity within the #HipHopEd family. We learned that good tweets have the same characteristics of classic rap lines. They are, as rap icon GZA describes, "half long, twice strong." More specifically, the best #HipHopEd tweeters are :

– *Concise*: able to express your thoughts within the space allotted
– *Creative*: able to be imaginative while expressing your voice through your tweet
– *Critical*: able to bring insight that questions power and brings new ideas
– *Consistent*: able to repeatedly offer effective tweets throughout a given chat session

When one effectively implements these four Cs into their #HipHopEd tweets, the larger community responds through retweets, favorites and comments. The ideas from the tweets take on a life of their own and grow beyond the chat. #HipHopEd chat are often retweeted and marked as favorites for hours and sometimes even days after the chat, and we often get follow up tweets based on what has happened in real life based on the tweets that were sent. This continued "tweet life" is international, and evident in the number of people from across the globe who join the #HipHopEd chat from different time zones. We have consistent participation from our constituents in the United Kingdom who are an estimated five hours ahead of Eastern Standard Time depending on the time of year. On many occasions, our constituents from the United Kingdom are chiming in between 2:00 am and 3:00 am so they can connect with the #HipHopEd family when the chat is live. While our family from Chile and Canada have contributed greatly to our work, the UK family (led by Darren Chetty @rapclassroom) constructed a manifesto a few years ago that served to bring together a vision and mission for the work in the UK that organically emerged from our chats.

While the impact of #HipHopEd as chat is far reaching and is almost impossible to accurately measure. There are various analytic applications that allow you to measure the reach of your tweets and the amount of tweets that were posted in a given time. Twitter also will deem hash tags as trending

MOST OF MY HEROES DONT APPEAR IN THE NATIONAL CURRICULUM

A HIPHOPED MANIFESTO
WE BELIEVE...

HIPHOPED CAN, MUST AND WILL BE MORE INCLUSIVE THAN EDUCATION AND HIPHOP
COLLABORATION IS AT THE HEART OF HIPHOP AND EDUCATION
MUCH THAT IS HIPHOP DOES NOT DECLARE ITSELF AS THUS
WE WILL TEACH ABOUT HIPHOP AND THROUGH HIPHOP

PEACE, UNITY, LOVE AND HAVING FUN
4 ELEMENTS PLUS KNOWLEDGE
MCs MODEL COURAGE – MAKE CYPHERS MOULD COMMUNITY
HIPHOP IS A DIALOGUE
TEACHER EAR IS AS IMPORTANT AS PUPIL VOICE
MICROPHONES AMPLIFY PUPIL VOICE
YA DONT STOP...LEARNING
HIPHOP IS MULTI-DISCIPLINARY AND CROSS-ARTS
CULTURAL PRODUCTION IS MORE VITAL THAN CONSUMPTION
SAMPLING CULTURE IS AN INTEGRAL PART OF THE CREATIVE PROCESS
CREATE SOMETHING OUT OF NOTHING – SOMETHING NEW OUT OF SOMETHING OLDER
BY CREATING WE BECOME OURSELVES
ALWAYS BE CREATING
WE ARE INSPIRED BY THE HIPHOP COMMUNITY OVER THE HIPHOP INDUSTRY
HIPHOP IS A FOLK ART
BUILDING CONFIDENCE BY SKILL AND VICE VERSA
GOOD TEACHERS COMBINE WRITTENS WITH COMING OFF THE TOP OF THE HEAD
THE CYPHER - CREATIVE CRITICAL COLLABORATIVE CARING COGENERATIVE
WE RECOGNISE DOMINANT CULTURE CO-OPTS OUTSIDER CULTURE FOR ITS OWN ENDS
WE REFUSE TO WALK AWAY

FIGURE 1.1   *#HipHopEdUK manifesto created by the #HipHopEd community in the United Kingdom.*

topics based on its overall activity over a given period of time. We have trended locally and internationally a number of times, and some of our chat activity has been the source of local news stories. IN these cases, we often convert the chat history into a transcript and posted it on Twitter as a resource for those who participated in the chat and others who may not have been able to participate. The transcripts are created using an application called "Chirpstory" and the views (or every time the link is opened) are counted.

The true impact of #HipHopEd is the relationships that have been established through the chat. On a number of occasions, the chat has brought people together who are doing work within a given locale, but didn't know one another. The chat has also served as an opportunity for work in progress like lesson plans and curriculum to be shared with constructive critiques provided by scholars within the community. The weekly chat has become a refuge for many educators who see hip-hop as education. It has recharged folks, taught them new strategie, and made their practice more successful. Lastly, and probably most importantly the #HipHopEd chat provides opportunities for cross generational dialogue to take place in a way that does not privilege the voice of adults, and provides opportunities for the youth to actively engage.

We see the weekly #HipHopEd chat as an online meeting space for real life revolutionaries. We see it as the contemporary digital version of the meeting room at the University of Natal when the South African Students Association plotted to find their voice under a repressive Apartheid regime. It is a universal space that welcomes all that use hip-hop as a form of voice. We engage, empower, and arm #HipHopEd(ucators) with the tools to do real work in schools and the community and support them in pushing back against the narratives that have been told about them by schools and society. We validate the resilient and powerful teenage mother whose story had been disfigured and re-carved into welfare queen, the Muslim student whose story has been distorted to become terrorist, the elderly activist grandmother whose passion for change has been skewed into "too old" or out of touch. We say that because they respond to the boom bap of hip-hop instrumentals, respond to the beauty of graffiti art, respect the technical wizardry of the DJ and heed the words of a true MC, that they are intellectual giants that need their seat at the education table. They are the insiders within the communities they are embedded in, and have the most powerful impact on what happens within their schools and their communities once they can consistently be refueled and empowered during the weekly chat.

3   On Hierarchies and Scholarship

#HipHopEd(ucators) communicate across platforms and boundaries created by degrees, grades being taught, academic position, or title. We engage in forms of coalition building where the academic, the teacher, and the everyday hip-hop enthusiast are not separated from each other or positioned in hierarchies that place more or less value on contributors based on some arbitrary criteria constructed by institutions that only serve to weaken our connections to each other and strengthen themselves. We work to ensure that the professors among us are not identified as the only producers of knowledge, and that the expertise of each of our stakeholders is consistently showcased. #HipHopEd rejects the notion that the "academic" should be creating the information for the teachers and the teachers should producing all the knowledge for the students. This is why this volume has contributors from high school students, graduate students, hip-hop artists, K-12 educators, youth development practitioners, out of school time educators, and college professors. The knowledge that is created/generated here is shared in efforts to display a model that values all that contribute while advancing our collective knowledge.

While the creation of a book is usually perceived as the end goal for scholars who engage in some type of shared academic work, for contributors here, it is just a first of many volumes to come, and another small piece of the work that we will continue to do both online and offline.

PART 1

Our Philosophy as Pedagogy

∵

Tweets

∵

 Edmund Adjapong
@KingAdjapong

A successful MC is exudes confidence at all
times when on stage. Educators must be
confident in their delivery of content
#HipHopEd

 Timothy Jones
@kij6899

MCs perform the same song in various
settings & adjust 2 the crowd. Teachers
must teach the same content w/variety
#HipHopEd

Jon Balcerak
@ JonBalcerak

A teacher/MC must be able 2 freestyle,
which is 2 say: think on one's feet,
communicate creatively, different 4 every
performance #HipHopEd

Shane Tate
@EducatorTate

#HipHopEd Real recognizes real. MCs who
do it well are ones who keep reality and
realness at center, something the
"educator" must do

 StraightOuttaHipHop
@So_hiphop

To me, a great MC empowers the listener. A
great teacher provides lessons to empower
students.

Introduction to Part 1: Philosophy as Pedagogy

Christopher Emdin and Timothy Jones
@ChrisEmdin and @Tdj6899

Any study of hip-hop that goes beyond a search through commercial radio hits, uncovers that participants in the culture consistently reflect on, and provide a powerful critique of formal education. Despite the grossly inaccurate grand narratives about the anti-academic identities of participants in hip-hop in media (Patton et al., 2009), youth in hip-hop consistently provides a powerful analysis of schools and schooling (Ginwright, 2004; Emdin, 2016). From the 1970's till present, hip-hop, rappers like Grandmaster flash, Biggie, Hopsin, Meek Mill and Migos have made references to teachers who told them "they wouldn't amount to nothin" or wouldn't make it in life. Artists like Kanye West have provided in-depth critiques of schools and schooling that specifically addresses both the experiences of youth in schools and the challenges of those who have graduated from school with little to nothing to show for it. These artists speak to the experiences of a generation of young people who feel alienated and disempowered within institutions that are culturally disconnected from who they are once they leave schools. It is in response to this lack of voice that hip-hop not only provides an analysis and critique of schools, but concurrently reimagines what schools and schooling can and should look like. The chapters in this part are based on the fundamental understanding that hip-hop provides powerful exemplars for what it means to be a revolutionary educator. In many ways, each of the authors provide an example of what teachers can do once they begin to understand what hip-hop means for teaching and learning.

In her chapter, Gloria Ladson Billings (GLB) brilliantly makes the connections between culturally relevant pedagogy and positions herself as an OG (a seasoned veteran) among educational researchers who are part of the #HipHopEd community. This positioning of/as O.G. is powerful because of the ways that hip-hop has been positioned as youth culture. and the ways that #HipHopEd functions to redefine it in ways that not only creates a space for elders, but positions them as significant to the growth of the culture. We bring O.G's like GLB into a literary cypher with mid-career and junior scholars Bettina Love and Courtney Rose and do so to showcase the power of #HipHopEd's model of inclusiveness within our ranks and in our public work. and and how, in many ways, #HipHopEd builds on the concept of culturally relevant pedagogy.

© KONINKLIJKE BRILL NV, LEIDEN, 2018 | DOI 10.1163/9789004371873_002

Gloria Ladson Billings reminds us that #HipHopEd(ucators) must engage in their work with a critical consciousness informed by youth and youth culture. This critical consciousness is what Courtney Rose argues for in her exploration of what is needed to train educators to use Critical Hip-hop Pedagogy (CHHP) in the classroom. Her exploration of preparing teachers to be hip-hop educators through enacting a Critical Hip-hop Pedagogy is integral to preparing educators to be effective in teaching the hip-hop generation. Courtney Rose pulls from her experiences as an elementary school teacher to highlight the fact that far too many educators who work with students from the hip-hop generation do not feel adequately prepared to teach them. Her research on preparing teachers to be critical hip-hop pedagogues gives insight into a new frontier in #HipHopEd and will change the landscape of urban education in years to come. Finally, Bettina Love introduces KRS-One and uses his role as teacher to articulate a number of points about our larger theme.

KRS-ONE, who is one of the greatest MC's in hip-hop, calls himself "The Teacher" and in his recordings, performances, and lectures, consistently provides a model for what teaching should look like. His identity as teacher takes on new forms in each project he releases and each performance/presentation he delivers to the public (Parmar, 2009). The KRS in KRS-ONE stands for "Knowledge Reigns Supreme" and through his name and his identity as teacher, he showcases the power and significance of teaching as gaining new knowledge. KRS-ONE moves educators to the recognition that the new knowledge gained from studying with the youth is the premiere goal of the educator. In the contemporary era, artists like Kendrick Lamar take on this role of teacher as they disseminate new knowledge, challenge systems, and do so while maintaining their hip-hop authenticity.

Each of the chapters in this part describe the potential that hip-hop has for giving educators new insight into improving schools and schooling through a hip-hop lens. They lead educators, researchers and community members to an understanding of underexplored questions within hip-hop and education that push the culture forward. Some of those questions are specific and connect to particular content areas and elements of hip-hop, while others are more broad and exploratory. Questions like what can be taught through graffiti art in the classroom? Can graffiti be used to teach the color wheel and primary colors? Can the angles and shapes within graffiti pieces be used to teach about angles and properties of shapes in geometry classes? Merge with questions like, what approaches/strategies that have been applied successfully in education using hip-hop? And what tools exist for educators and stakeholders in hip-hop to develop their own applications of hip-hop pedagogy.

As you read the chapters within this part, reflect on your views of hip-hop music and culture. Your views will impact the way you process the larger philosophy of #HipHopEd and hip-hop pedagogy. As Christopher Emdin, Timothy Jones, Gloria Ladson Billings, Bettina Love, and Courtney Rose suggest, employ critical consciousness as you read this part and glean from it powerful insight into the nature of hip-hop pedagogy.

References

Emdin, C. (2016). *For White folks who teach in the hood ... and the rest of y'all too: Reality pedagogy and urban education*. Boston, MA: Beacon Press.

Ginwright, S. (2004). *Black in school: Afrocentric reform, urban youth, and the promise of hip-hop culture*. New York, NY: Teachers College Press.

Parmar, P. (2009). *Knowledge reigns supreme: The critical pedagogy of hip-hop artist KRS-ONE*. Rotterdam, The Netherlands: Sense Publishers.

Paton, J., Crouch, W., & Camic, P. (2009). Young offenders' experiences of traumatic life events: A qualitative investigation. *Clinical Child Psychology and Psychiatry, 14*, 43–62.

CHAPTER 1

From Big Homie the O.G., to GLB: Hip-hop and the Reinvention of a Pedagogue

Gloria Ladson-Billings
@gjladson

> *I – I – I am everyday people!*
> SLY & THE FAMILY STONE/ARRESTED DEVELOPMENT

I will admit that I am an odd choice to be found in the middle of the pedagogical revolution that hip-hop education is producing. Indeed, when the Sugar Hill Gang released the iconic, "Rapper Delight," I had already graduated from college, earned a Master's degree, taught 10 years in a big urban school district, and was sitting in graduate school pursuing a Ph.D. I was more Motown than Master P; more Mary Wells than Mary J; more O'Jays than Jay-Z. But, somehow hip-hop has captivated me in ways that force me to re-evaluate my work and how I relate to students.

I am known as a "pedagogical theorist" which is a fancy way to say that I think deeply and seriously about the art and craft of teaching. I research teaching. I study teaching. And, I experiment with teaching in an attempt to improve my own teaching and the teaching that occurs in classrooms serving African American students. My specific focus on African American students has to do with the ways they have been so marginalized and disrespected in schools and classrooms.

Twenty-five years ago, I began researching the pedagogical practices of teachers who were successful with African American children. I chose this issue because after 5 years at one of the nation's most prestigious universities I kept hearing how "nobody" had demonstrated academic success with Black children. So ingrained is this notion that all of the literature I searched reinforced it. My first electronic searches using descriptors like, "Black Education" and "African American Education" quickly defaulted to cross references that read, "see culturally deprived," or "see cultural deficits." The language of academic excellence was absent when it came to considering African American children. Thus, my work became more than locating what I would later call, "existence proofs" – evidence that there were teachers capable of fostering academic success among African American students – rather, crafting a theoretical

© KONINKLIJKE BRILL NV, LEIDEN, 2018 | DOI 10.1163/9789004371873_003

platform on which to build this kind of expertise so that it would become more widely distributed and celebrated. I developed a theory I called, "culturally relevant pedagogy" (Ladson-Billings, 1995a/2009, 1995b).

Today, I hear the term, "culturally relevant pedagogy" everywhere I go. Unfortunately, the practices I see rarely represent the practice I described when I had the opportunity to spend 3 years with 8 outstanding teachers. So, I will briefly describe what I meant by culturally relevant pedagogy (CRP) when I began to explicate these successful teachers' work. CRP involves 3 main components: a focus on student learning, developing students' cultural competence, and critical consciousness. Student learning may seem an obvious component but here I am referring to the intellectual growth that students experience as a result of the experiences they have in the school, community, and classroom especially with the help of a skilled teacher. I am not merely referencing "gain scores" on standardized measures that are typically separate and disconnected from the curriculum.

The second component is cultural competence. I think of this as the "misunderstood" aspect of CRP. As someone trained in anthropology I have a deep sense of what is meant by the term, "culture." It involved every aspect of human endeavor including thought, perceptions, feelings, and attitudes. It is not merely the tangible components of a community such as artifacts, foods, and customs – although those things are indeed a part of culture. However, it is important to emphasize the dynamic and fluid nature of culture that is much more than lists of "central tendencies" or worse, "cultural stereotypes."

In many of today's human services professionals use the term "cultural competence." Thus, we hear of culturally competent nursing, culturally competent counseling, or culturally competent policing. Unfortunately, much of what I have read and seen of these practices consists of using a list of "do's and don'ts" in dealing with clients who racial, ethnic or linguistic groups different from the mainstream. This limited perspective on culture almost always conceives of culture as static, unchanging sets of actions or behaviors. In the context of culturally relevant pedagogy cultural competence refers to the skill and facility to help students recognize and appreciate their cultural of origin while also learning to develop fluency in at least one other culture.

This definition has several important dimensions. First it implies that all students have culture (whether they are aware of it or not) and that their culture is a valuable, indeed necessary, starting point for learning. Cognitive psychologists insist that prior knowledge is crucial for learning. Those linguistic tools, thoughts, and ways of being that students come to school with are foundational for their learning. Second, this definition of cultural competence points out that ALL students should be able to develop fluency in at least one other culture – even those who are members of the mainstream.

The third component of culturally relevant pedagogy is socio political (or critical) consciousness. This component is the most often ignored element of CRP. In plain English it might be thought of as the "so what" factor. Year after year our students ask us why they have to learn certain things. They want to know what good is school knowledge. Unfortunately, we typically offer weak responses such as, "You're going to need this information next year!" Most students recognize early on that answer is not true. Some will be compliant because they recognize the credentialing value of schooling but far too many dismiss school as irrelevant and disengage to their own detriment.

Culturally relevant teachers work hard to help students engage in meaningful projects that solve problems that matter in their lives. They also work to help students develop a critical consciousness that allows them to question the veracity of what they read in classrooms and pose powerful questions about social, cultural, economic, political, and other problems of living in a democracy that attempts to serve a diverse populace.

1   The R(e)volution of Culturally Relevant Pedagogy

Over 25 years ago when I began researching the practice of exemplary teachers of African American students I had no idea this work would consume my scholarly life. But, the road I traveled down a quarter of a century ago has taken me to an exciting and surprising point. I began to realize that the way many of the teachers I worked with deployed culture in their classrooms was to pull upon the established, historic aspects of students' culture. The teachers were concerned that conventional textbooks and mandated curriculum rarely included the histories of students who were not a part of the dominant culture. And, I must say the CRP teachers I first documented did a marvelous job of increasing students' knowledge and pride of their history, heritage, and culture.

However, what I began to recognize was missing from the work was any attention to youth culture. Almost everyone who was working on youth culture at the time was working in out of school and community based settings. I realized that we were missing an important part of what mattered to students – their own, organic, self-generated culture. And, what a culture it was! Students' expression of their identities showed up in their dress, their language, their dance, their art, their fascination and facility with technology, and above all their music. The melding and mixing of strong breakbeats with incredible lyrics delivered at staccato, rapid-fire rates signified a new way to think about and conceive of music and schools and classrooms were missing out on all of this.

Of course, as these new youth culture forms were developing I was living in the academy. I worked with students who had already demonstrated their ability to master the standard curriculum. For the most part, that mastery is what got them into the university. However, it was clear that as I worked to prepare the next generation of teachers our teacher preparation program had some serious shortcomings. Despite being heralded as a top program we struggled to attract a diverse prospective teacher cohort and nothing in our program was addressing the way new forms of youth culture could influence and promote student learning.

Coincident with learning more about youth culture I also learned that students from our campus' award-winning "First Wave Hip-hop and Urban Arts Learning Community" regularly started our teacher education program but rarely completed it. The First Wave students felt that sitting in classes with 24 White, middle income mostly females from suburban or rural Wisconsin was not the best way to learn to teach in the urban centers they wanted to return to. First Wave students typically came from Milwaukee, Chicago, New York, Detroit, and other major urban centers. They were students who survived schools and communities that were difficult but taught them resilience and perseverance. They were not merely survivors; they were thrivers. And, because many of them were determined to go back into their home communities and work as educators to ensure that more students like themselves would have a fair shot at getting a real education and being productive in their communities and beyond.

The First Wave director, Willie Ney and I sat down to talk about possible solutions to the students' concerns. My first strategy was to help the students develop what our campus calls, "Independent majors" where we could hand pick a suite of courses that better suited their needs. However, what I learned is that many of the students continued to pursue their dream of teaching despite not earning teacher certification. Thus, many of the students ended up in alternative teacher certification programs like Teach for America or City Year. Because I knew that these programs rarely prepare young people to work in the challenging environments in which they are placed, I agreed to design a course that would provide some rudimentary preparation for thinking about teaching and merging youth culture, i.e., hip-hop.

The first course I developed was titled, "Pedagogy, Performance, and Culture." It was designed as an introduction to education course that looked at the social foundations of education and the social foundations of hip-hop. With the aid of a little money we were able to pair the course with a public lecture series where we would invite scholars, artists, and activists to give a lecture to the larger campus community and spend time interacting one on one with the students enrolled in the course. We were careful not to make it just a First Wave course by holding half of the seats for students who were not a part of their urban arts community. For one thing I wanted to be careful not to "ghettoize" the experience and for another, I wanted the non-artists/performers to experience what it meant to learn with and from students whose experiences were vastly different from their own.

I began the first session with an activity called "Where I'm from" which is a take-off of a poem by George Ella Lyon. I gave each student a few minutes to create a spoken word piece to would introduce them to the rest of the class. True to my usual way of working, I too created a piece. In my piece I included a hook that goes, "You know me, I'm GLB; You know me, I'm GLB." From that moment, that's who I became to the students – GLB. The work we did together helped me to embrace this new identity. Could I literally function as an MC in this new teaching format? Could a Big Homie and OG become GLB?

We called the public lecture series "Getting Real 2" to keep it consistent with a previous series the Office of Multicultural Arts Initiatives had hosted. Our guests included hip-hop filmmaker Eli Jacob-Fantauzzi whose films, "Inventos: Hip-hop Cubanos" and "Homegrown: Hip-Life in Ghana" explore the global spread and influence of hip-hop. We later had cultural studies scholar, Mark Anthony Neal (Duke University) who talked about hip-hop, wealth and social justice. This talk challenged us to think about whether moguls and stars like Jay-Z and Kanye West actually were engaged in some form of social justice. We followed up with lectures by Dawn Elissa Fisher, the "Def Professor (San Francisco State University) and her co-worker, the infamous, "Davey D" who shared what it meant to do community-based teaching as well as some of the behind the scene machinations of the commercial radio business. Our next guest was Professor Elaine Richardson a.k.a. Docta E (Ohio State University). She was the first of our guest lecturers to actually perform along with sharing her research interests of working with middle school girls in out of school contexts. We then had Anna West, a youth spoken word organizer who many of the Chicago based students knew from the "Louder than a Bomb!" poetry slam competition. In our next week we were scheduled to have linguist, H. Samy Alim (Stanford University) but he was too ill to fly. Instead, we did a Skype with Samy in our classroom and were fortunate enough to be able to host Christopher Emdin. Chris' exploration of hip-hop and urban science was a fabulous presentation that culminated with a mini-freestyle battle between Chris and 3 of the First Wave students. In the remaining weeks we hosted Marc Lamont Hill (Morehouse, CNN, Huffington Post Live, BET), Martha Diaz and Eddie Fergus (NYU), David Stovall (University of Illinois-Chicago), and Chris Walker (University of Wisconsin-Madison) who serves as the artistic director for First Wave.

In the culminating activity for the students I had originally planned for the First Wave students to develop performance pieces and the non-First Wave students would develop some type of curriculum project. However, about a third of the way through the semester I determined it would be a more challenging learning experience for all of the students to participate in the performance. All students would be a part of a small group that would conceptualize, write, and perform a piece on stage before an audience. I offered the students the option of having me assign the group membership or doing it themselves. My only stipulation was that every group had to comprised of both First Wave and non-First Wave students. The students wanted to select their own groups and they did a fair and equitable job of balancing the composition of the groups.

On the evening of the final cypher the students presented 5 pieces that merged the educational research we studied with spoken word, dance, and hip-hop. Some of the skits employed humor and some focused on very serious themes of disparity, inequity, injustice, education, and pedagogy. The students merged the research and the art in powerful ways. It was exciting to see the non-performers push themselves and feel that giddy nervousness and adrenaline rush of standing before an audience. Their comments afterward were, "I've never been so scared in my whole life but I've never felt more alive!"

One of the students was from a suburban Milwaukee community and I confess I always had an eye out for her because I assumed she would be crushed by the fact that her experiences and knowledge were so limited compared to many of the other students. But, I also saw her working hard to understand and learn. She probably had the steepest mountain to climb in the course but climb it she did. Today she is a teacher in a nearby community but I notice that she regularly attends First Wave events and hip-hop performances. She talks easily and readily about how hip-hop informs her teaching and opened up her thinking.

But, I was the person who learned the most from this experience. I was forced to read, study, and work to learn about the way aspects of hip-hop fit this theoretical concept I termed, Culturally Relevant Pedagogy. I learned that the work of learning culture applied to me also. I had to learn how to reinvent my practice in the context of new cultural forms and cultural practices. I had to be willing to r(e)volutionize culturally relevant pedagogy.

References

Ladson-Billings, G. (1995a/2009). *The dreamkeepers: Successful teachers of African American children*. San Francisco, CA: Jossey Bass.

Ladson-Billings, G. (1995b). Toward a theory of culturally relevant pedagogy. *American Educational Research Journal, 32*, 465–491.

CHAPTER 2

Toward a Critical Hip-hop Pedagogy for Teacher Education

Courtney Rose
@IvyRose67

My first introduction to the enactment of hip-hop culture *as* pedagogy occurred in my last semester of classes while working on my Masters at the Harvard Graduate School of Education (HGSE). I had one remaining elective course requirement to fill so I took a course on understanding global hip-hop identities. I decided to use this opportunity to venture onto the main campus, enrolling in a course on international hip-hop identities. Having an opportunity to understand personal struggles in identity development attracted me to anything involving an explicit exploration of the topic. I figured it would at the very least be a fun and interesting note on which to close out my time as a Harvard graduate student. The class was held in Harvard's newly opened Hip-hop Archive & Research Institute. The walls were covered with images of African American musicians, actors and their work (movie posters, album art, etc.). The space in which the actual instruction was performed was almost the complete antithesis of the antiquated, White-washed spaces I had come to expect from higher learning institutions, particularly Harvard.

Although school was always a space in which I experienced academic success, never before had I been so connected to academic content. On a daily basis we were asked to "come as who we were" and to truly think about how constructions of our identities (both our own and those others/society imposed upon us) shape our experiences while our experiences simultaneously shaped who we were. Together we explored the nuances of society, breaking down explicit and implicit messages of privilege, access, oppression and constructions of race, gender, and sexuality while always taking a moment to reflect on how we were positioned. It was a communal study of individual identities where each person felt supported in the discomfort of exploring the ways in which "who we were" in various spaces disrupted and in some cases reproduced the conditions for inequities to persist. Engaging in this level of critical analysis helped me find a new voice accompanied with a surprising sense of freedom and hope. I began to acknowledge the ways I played a role in my own *oppression* through the conscious and unconscious *suppression* of

© KONINKLIJKE BRILL NV, LEIDEN, 2018 | DOI 10.1163/9789004371873_004

various parts of my identity in an effort to "fit in" and adjust to my surroundings. Through this process of continued reflection and analysis I could easily see that I had within me the power to *take action* toward change.

1   Falling in Line

I carried this experience with me as I entered the classroom taking on the official title/role of "teacher." Armed with the language of culturally relevant education, I developed a classroom vision around the goals of *high academic achievement* and the development of a *critical consciousness* that would foster a sense of urgency and a path to action leading my students to disrupt the status quo (Ladson-Billings, 1995). Noting my students' attraction to and engagement with rap and hip-hop, and remembering the transformative experience from my course at Harvard, I attempted to recreate that space. As a Math/Science teacher I struggled to find ways to integrate some of the practices of my professor who taught the course on global hip-hop identities., unsure of where the work needed to start with my fifth graders. I finally settled on beginning with the use of rap as a hook to engage my students, looking to canned programs that used rap to teach students various skills such as multiplication and division tables. While initially this worked as a means to draw them in, it did very little to keep them engaged. I quickly began to feel the pressure of meeting demands amidst time constraints, mandates on the use of scripted curriculum and random administrative observations within the increasingly test-based competition-driven culture of my school (and public school culture at large). Feeling exhausted and unsupported, I abandoned my vision and did my best to fall in line with school, district and statewide requirements.

I find it difficult to reflect on my first year of teaching as it forces me to come face-to-face with the ways in which I believe I failed my students. It would be easy to place the blame solely on the culture of schools in which conforming to standardized practices designed around the social norms of society comes in direct conflict with many educators' attempts at creating spaces that require and value culturally-specific ways of knowing and expressing knowledge (Nasaw, 1979; Kliebard, 2004). Unquestionably, these structural issues play a major part in teachers' perceptions of their abilities to effectively engage in critical culturally responsive practices, and I think it is important for educators to acknowledge and name these potential constraints and barriers. However, I approach my current work and research with the stance that as "teacher" I played a central role in reinforcing and validating the barriers to enacting such praxis within the context of my classroom. Therefore, examining the shortcomings of my attempts to transform teaching and learning with and for students always begins with the exploration of my own beliefs and actions.

2 Shifting Focus

Early on in my doctoral studies, remaining grounded in this process of critical self-analysis, I found myself intrigued by the theoretical conceptualizations presented by critical hip-hop pedagogues (CHHP) (e.g. Akom, 2009; Emdin, 2013; Adjapong, 2017). These scholars' work look to similar arguments presented in the foundations of other critical approaches to multicultural education in the development of practices that centralize culturally-diverse students' voices and experiences as a means of disrupting and dismantling the status quo (Akom, 2009). Noting hip-hop's function as a vehicle of self-expression and resistance among urban Black and Latino/a youth, these pedagogues understand hip-hop to be a means through which to expose and critique social inequities, particularly in relation to access to opportunities within education (Akom, 2009).

Over time, my research interests shifted from transforming practices at the K-12 classroom level to transforming the curricular designs and pedagogical approaches utilized within teacher education programs. I began researching and examining various enactments of CHHP within higher education and specifically with pre- and in-service teachers seeking to disrupt dominant discourses about valuable topics of and approaches to instruction. Expanding on the knowledge base provided by previous iterations of Hip-hop Based Education (HHBE), CHHP scholarship has unearthed the ways in which knowledge of and participation in hip-hop cultural practices can serve as both a form of cultural capital and a resource for racial and generational identity formation (Dimitriadis, 2001; Hill, 2009a). With this in mind, self-proclaimed critical hip-hop pedagogues call for an expansion within the field of HHBE from an emphasis on *teaching with hip-hop texts (i.e. rap songs)* to *teaching with hip-hop sensibilities and aesthetics*. Doing so allows for deeper engagement with the other dimensions of hip-hop culture (DJing, graffiti/visual art, fashion, spoken word/poetry, etc.) to create educational environments that embody more complex and genuine representations of hip-hop culture (Akom, 2009; Alim, 2007; Williams, 2009).

Below, I provide a breakdown of the four common elements that surface among prominent scholars and pedagogues as commonly held stances and tenets that guide recent iterations of CHHP. In shifting the lens from teacher practice to teacher preparation I offer these as a framework for Critical Hip-hop Teacher Education (CHHTE) in the transformation of curricular designs and instructional practices in the preparation of teachers for *all* students.

3   Understanding Hip-hop as Lived Experience/Identity

The first tenet of CHHP serves as its foundation, emphasizing the need to recognize hip-hop as lived experience. Hip-hop scholars, historians and pedagogues challenge reductionist rap-centric approaches that relegate hip-hop to consumption during out-of-school and/or leisure time to a more comprehensive representation of hip-hop as a way of coming to know and be in the world (Akom, 2009; Alridge, 2005; Emdin, 2010). In this regard hip-hop pedagogues hold the stance that many of today's urban youth use hip-hop cultural artifacts and practices to "seek meaning, acceptance and belonging" (Williams, 2009, p. 2) and as such is an invaluable cultural lens through which educators can engage students in an educational process aimed at social justice and the development of a critical consciousness (Emdin, 2010).

4   Dialogic Problem-Posing Curriculum

The second tenet of CHHP pulls explicitly from its theoretical grounding in Freirean critical pedagogy. Proponents of CHHP view students' lived experiences *as* knowledge and therefore problematize the traditional approach to education that constructs students as empty vessels into which educators must deposit information (Emdin, 2013; Williams, 2009). This approach, which Freire (1986) termed the "banking method" ignores and devalues students' prior experiences, skills and knowledge thus highly limiting their ability to act as agents in the teaching and learning process. Engagement in this dialogic process requires educators to shift from lecturer to facilitator, centering students' voices and experiences and disrupting the culture of socialization and domestication inherent in traditional models of schooling (Freire, 1986; Smith-Maddox & Solorzano, 2002). Through the enactment of dialogic pedagogy both students and educators are able to take more active roles in the teaching and learning process, leading to the liberation of oppressor and oppressed through the shifting dynamics in student-teacher social relations (Smith-Maddox & Solorzano, 2002). Much of Freire's work served to address issues of illiteracy, which he directly.

Hip-hop scholars, historians and pedagogues linking the bi-directional dialogic processes of Freire's culture circles to practices within hip-hop culture find that it strongly mirrors practices associated with the hip-hop cypher (Emdin, 2013; Newman, 2005; Williams, 2009). Cypher participants, usually emcees (rappers) or bboys/girls (dancers), form a circle and take turns showcasing their skills in a freestyle (improvisational) fashion. Each participant is expected to participate in the cypher by contributing something to the "performance" (Emdin, 2013; Newman, 2005; Williams, 2009). In both Freire's culture circles and hip-hop's cyphers the circle represents a disruption of hierarchical positioning as participants stand equidistant of each other encouraging dialogue/participation as all participants are on equal ground. Additionally, as each participant contributes to the dialogue or performance the piece becomes more dynamic as participants are pushed in their thinking and performers are encouraged to bring forth their best skills in order to enhance the experience (Emdin, 2013).

The majority of applications of the dialogic process has been applied to the acquisition of literacy skills, as this is often the most conducive space for educators to see opportunities to incorporate associated practices. However, the need to address the lack of representation of Black and Latino/a students in STEM-related courses and fields has led to greater focus on how to apply hip-hop based dialogic practices in these subject-areas (Hill & Petchauer, 2013). Emdin (2013) draws attention to the science-mindedness that exists within the enactment of hip-hop elements. Of particular importance to Emdin is the emphasis within hip-hop culture on the co-construction of knowledge and co-development of practice, which mirrors exactly Freire's (1970) call for educators to work in tandem with students in the teaching and learning process. Emdin (2011) applies many of the same practices associated with Freire's problem-posing model as he maps out strategies for restructuring traditional science classrooms that more effectively engage urban youth identifying with hip-hop culture.

The *reality pedagogy* model and Freire's (1970) *problem-posing praxis* model each engage students and teachers in a collaborative dialogic process aimed at bridging students' out-of-school experiences and identities with their academic experiences and identities and goals. Through these dialogic processes, students and teachers collectively identify issues of importance that impact and/or shape the daily functioning of the classroom, school community or surrounding neighborhood and co-create the subsequent curricular activities, pedagogical practices and/or activities necessary to address the identified issues. At the core of these processes are Freire's concept of *conscientizacao* and reality pedagogues' conceptualization of cosmopolitanism, or "a way of knowing and being that embraces a belief in human responsibility for each other and of the value of the individual differences" (Emdin, 2011, p. 290). Through engagement in such processes, the goal is for students and educators to develop a sense of shared identity and responsibility in addressing issues that shape the environments and conditions in which teaching and learning take place.

5   Curriculum as (De)Colonizer

The third major tenet of CHHP also pulls from its roots in critical theories (i.e. Critical Race Theory, critical pedagogy, and critical culturally relevant/ responsive pedagogy). These scholars frame discussions of curricular and educational reform efforts in the belief that teaching and learning are political acts and cannot be neutral (Goodwin, 2010). To these scholars, the decisions educators make in the development and implementation of their pedagogical practices shed light on their ideological beliefs about the purposes and functions of schools. Specifically, critical pedagogues emphasize the manner in which various institutions of society are structured to (re)produce inequalities through the socialization of citizens under normalized and institutionalized ideas about what is acceptable and preferred in society (Goodwin, 2010).

Similarly, acknowledging the quick growth of an increasingly diverse population, proponents of CHHP echo calls for the development and implementation of practices that do more than function as a bridge between home and school that is eventually burned once students assimilate into dominant social norms. Critical hip-hop scholars/pedagogues posit that CHHP provides a counter-curriculum that challenges the myths, presuppositions and supposed wisdoms of the official curriculum (Akom, 2009; Emdin, 2010). Existing literature on hip-hop pedagogy points to the necessity for educators working with urban youth identifying with hip-hop culture to gain understanding of the often oppositional discourses inherent within hip-hop culture and the inherently deficit-based discourses that frame many practices and policies within traditional public schooling. This understanding can assist educators to identify sites of possibilities through which to challenge traditional paradigms, texts, and theories used to explain the experiences of racially, culturally, linguistically, and socioeconomically diverse students (Hill, 2009; Pulido, 2009; Sealey-Ruiz & Greene, 2010).

Youth identifying and engaging with hip-hop culture face continuous alienation from and within traditional school environments. Schools often serve as sites for ideological battles in which these students consistently find their out-of-school ways of thinking, communicating, knowing and being labeled as deficient and in need of remediation and correction (Alim & Pennycook, 2007; Emdin, 2010). However, critical hip-hop pedagogues disrupt such deficit-based mindsets through the incorporation of teaching and learning styles that welcome their out-of-school ways of knowing and being to thrive. Their shift from incorporation of hip-hop/urban youth culture as a bridge to the mainstream to an approach that values diverse representations and manifestations of knowledge and skills expands conventional conceptions of "smartness" and "goodness" creating opportunities for a greater number of students to achieve success. Specifically, existing literature reveals how enacting pedagogical practices grounded in hip-hop/urban youth culture enables students and teachers to negotiate and navigate conflicting explicit and implicit messages within society in order to develop positive academic and social identities through the inevitable repositioning that occurs as space is created for diverse voices and perspectives.

6   Toward a Development of Critical Consciousness

Continuing to look to the aims of other critical pedagogical approaches, proponents of CHHP state one of its primary aims as being the development of a critical consciousness that moves students and educators toward action for change (Akom, 2009; Williams, 2009). Broadly defined critical consciousness "represents the capacity to critically reflect and act upon one's social environment" (Diemer, Kauffman, Koenig, Trahan, & Hsieh, 2006, p. 445). Hip-hop scholars, historians and pedagogues look to the common practice within hip-hop of explicitly naming the daily injustices faced within traditionally marginalized, underserved and underrepresented low-income urban communities as a point of entry through which to begin critical work with students. Critical hip-hop pedagogues' exploration of hip-hop cultural language and social interactions, including rap lyrics and music serves as the appropriate starting point to begin naming the daily injustices experienced by urban youth and identify the context-specific problems that impact their students (Au, 2005).

Critical hip-hop pedagogues utilize both non-traditional texts (music videos, films, television series, songs, out-of-school experiences/personal narratives, etc.) and hip-hop aesthetics (sampling, battling, the cypher, schooling, etc.) to facilitate the deconstruction of "the veracity of dominant texts" (Gosa & Fields, 2012, p. 4). Through this process of deconstruction, which is grounded in bi-directional dialogue between student and teacher, the CHHP classroom holds potential as an emancipatory space in which both student and teacher are liberated from traditional standardized, assimilationist approaches.

Echoing other critical and culturally relevant theories for multicultural teacher education/development, proponents of CHHP find it necessary for educators to engage in continuous explicit critical dialogue and reflection about the intersections of race (and its intersections with other identity markers such as class, gender, and sexuality), social injustice, inequity and education. Looking to hip-hop's roots in politics and resistance as well as its prevalence within youth culture, critical hip-hop scholars and pedagogues posit that teaching though the cultural lens of hip-hop is conducive to the development of effective equity and social justice-oriented pedagogical practices that can begin to disrupt and dismantle existing power dynamics (Akom, 2009; Williams, 2009).

7   Conclusion

CHHP's emphasis on understanding students' lived experiences and culturally-defined frames of reference and utilizing them in the development of social-justice oriented curricular designs and instructional practices, places its proponents among those calling for the *transformation* of traditional university-based teacher education practices. Those holding this position share the emphasis on equity within the social justice education reform agenda (Zeichner, 2003) and often push for a reframing of discourses concerning the "achievement gap" to one of an "education debt" (Ladson-Billings, 2006), noting the cost of the historical and persistent narrative of difference as deficit that has pushed racially, culturally, linguistically and socio-economically diverse populations to the margins of society and educational policies, practices and curricular designs.

These factors are often overlooked when addressing necessary improvements to quality teacher education experiences, especially amidst seemingly well-intentioned efforts to improve accreditation standards through greater attention to the development of academic content knowledge and pedagogical/instructional skills (Zeichner, 2003). *Transformers'* dissatisfaction with the status quo in traditional teacher education program policies and practices results in a call for the development of stronger relationships and partnerships between colleges of education and the communities in which teachers are preparing to enter. Similarly, proponents of CHHP emphasize the need to disrupt and transform practices and policies rooted in assimilationist messages and traditional ideologies that frame cultural and social differences as deficits.

Recognizing educational institutions, as primary sites of the "construction, legitimation, and imposition" of dominant narratives and ideologies concerning what is *acceptable, truthful,* and *rewardable,* proponents of CHHP view these institutions as key locations within which to engage in ideological battles. It is within the highly charged political field of K-12 schools that traditionally marginalized students often find themselves in daily cultural combat (Alim, 2007). Thus educational institutions, including schools of education, may serve as appropriate locations to engage in processes of identifying, challenging and transforming damaging discourses and pedagogical practices in the development of social justice-oriented curricular designs and instructional practices framed by the lived experiences and realities of historically marginalized populations (Akom, 2009; Alim, 2007; Emdin, 2013).

Gaining a deeper understanding of the processes of teaching and learning within spaces specifically designed for the preparation of teachers who want to utilize hip-hop cultural artifacts and aesthetics to critical ends can provide insight into a potential model that works to address the unmet needs of pre-service teachers going into culturally diverse K-12 educational environments. Hip-hop's rise out of movements of social resistance by Black and Latino youth places at its core an emphasis on social justice and explicitly names societal and systemic problems related to race, class, gender, space/place and culture. Fusing these roots with the pedagogical and theoretical underpinnings of critical multicultural and culturally relevant approaches, CHHP "epistemologically and ontologically asks students to turn their gaze back toward the community and begin to solve problems by interrogating" the dominant discourses shaping their world(s) and their positionality within them (Akom, 2009). Additionally, CHHP's centering of traditionally marginalized and devalued ways of knowing and being in the world through hip-hop's emphasis on personal narratives humanizes teaching and learning while simultaneously (re)positioning students and teachers within traditional learning spaces (Akom, 2009; Hill & Petchauer, 2013; Williams, 2009). I posit that inherent within the roots of hip-hop culture lies the type of transformational "both/and" approach that stresses the importance of content/subject-matter knowledge as well as a need to name needed to disrupt damaging discourses of difference rooted in deficit-based ideologies so prevalent among traditional approaches to teacher education.

References

Adjapong, E. S. (2017). Bridging theory and practice in the urban science classroom: A framework for hip-hop pedagogy. *Critical Education, 8*(15), 5–23.

Akom, A. A. (2009). Critical hip-hop pedagogy as a form of liberatory praxis. *Equity & Excellence in Education, 42*(1), 52–66. doi:10.1080/10665680802612519

Alim, H. S. (2007). Critical hip-hop language pedagogies: Combat, consciousness, and the cultural politics of communication. *Journal of Language, Identity & Education, 6*(2), 161–176. doi:10.1080/15348450701341378

Alim, H. S., & Pennycook, A. (2007). Glocal linguistic flows: Hip-hop culture(s), identities, and the politics of language education. *Journal of Language, Identity & Education, 6*(2), 89–100. doi:10.1080/15348450701341238

Alridge, D. P., & Stewart, J. B. (2005). Introduction: Hip hop in history: Past, present, and future. *The Journal of African American History, 90*, 190–195. doi:10.2307/20063997

Au, W. (2005). Fresh out of school: Rap music's discursive battle with education. *The Journal of Negro Education, 74*(3), 210–220. doi:10.2307/40027428

Diemer, M. A., Kauffman, A., Koenig, N., Trahan, E., & Hsieh, C.-A. (2006). Challenging racism, sexism, and social injustice: Support for urban adolescents' critical consciousness development. *Cultural Diversity and Ethnic Minority Psychology, 12*(3), 444–460. doi:10.1037/1099-9809.12.3.444

Emdin, C. (2010). Urban science education for the hip-hop generation: Essential tools for the science educator and researcher. Rotterdam, The Netherlands: Sense Publishers.

Emdin, C. (2013). Pursuing the pedagogical potential of the pillars of hip-hop through Sciencemindedness. *International Journal of Critical Pedagogy, 4*(3), 83–99. Retrieved from http://libjournal.uncg.edu/ijcp/article/viewFile/352/438

Freire, P. (1986). *Pedagogy of the oppressed* (30th ed.). New York, NY: Continuum.

Goodwin, A. L. (2010). Curriculum as colonizer: (Asian) American education in the current U.S. context. *Teachers College Record, 112*(12), 3102–3138.

Gosa, T. L., & Fields, T. G. (2012). Is hip-hop education another hustle? The (ir)responsible use of hip-hop as pedagogy. In B. J. Porfilio & M. Viola (Eds.), *Hip-hop(e): The cultural practice and critical pedagogy of international hip-hop* (pp. 195–210). New York, NY: Peter Lang.

Hill, M. L. (2009). Wounded healing: Forming a storytelling community in hip-hop lit. *Teachers College Record, 111*(1), 248–293.

Hill, M. L., & Petchauer, E. (Eds.). (2013). *Schooling hip-hop: Expanding hip-hop based education across the curriculum.* New York, NY: Teachers College Press.

Ladson-Billings, G. (2006). From the achievement gap to the education debt: Understanding achievement in US schools. *Educational researcher, 35*(7), 3–12.

Newman, M. (2005). Rap as literacy: A genre analysis of hip-hop ciphers. *Text-Interdisciplinary Journal for the Study of Discourse, 25*(3), 399–436. doi:10.1515/text.2005.25.3.399

Paris, D., & Alim, H. S. (2014). What are we seeking to sustain through culturally sustaining pedagogy? A loving critique forward. *Harvard Educational Review, 84*(1), 85–100. doi:10.17763/haer.84.1.982l873k2ht16m77

Pulido, I. (2009). "Music fit for us minorities": Latinas/os' use of hip hop as pedagogy and interpretive framework to negotiate and challenge racism. *Equity & Excellence in Education, 42*(1), 67–85. doi:10.1080/10665680802631253

Sealey-Ruiz, Y., & Greene, P. (2010). Embracing urban youth culture in the context of education. *The Urban Review, 43*(3), 339–357. doi:10.1007/s11256-010-0156-8

Smith-Maddox, R., & Solórzano, D. G. (2002). Using critical race theory, Paulo Freire's problem-posing method, and case study research to confront race and racism in education. *Qualitative Inquiry, 8*(1), 66–84. doi:10.1177/1077800402008001005

Williams, D. A. (2009). The critical cultural cypher: Remaking Paulo Freire's cultural circles using hip hop culture. *International Journal of Critical Pedagogy, 2*(1), 1–29. Retrieved from http://www.freireproject.org/wp-content/journals/TIJCP/Vol2No1/282-682-1-PB.pdf

Zeichner, K. (2003). The adequacies and inadequacies of three current strategies to recruit, prepare and retain the best teachers for all students. *Teachers College Record, 105*(3), 490–519.

CHAPTER 3

Knowledge Reigns Supreme: The Fifth Element, Hip-hop Critical Pedagogy & Community

Bettina L. Love
@blovesoulpower

It seems to me in a school that's ebony, African history should be pumped up steadily, but it's not and this has to stop.

KRS-ONE, 1989

1 Stolen Legacy

The words above spoken by The Teacha, KRS-ONE, illustrate just how fundamental and crucial it is that African American children learn their remarkable history. In too many schools across the United States the rich history of African and African American people is disregarded, belittled, or suppressed in ways that depict African history as episodic (e.g., Black History Month) or detached from meaningful contributions that make today's world possible. According to Brown (2008), "[t]o acknowledge black people in voluntary transit runs the risk of affirming black people as historical agents, rather than as timeless people inextricably tied to the land and to a timeless past" (pp. 188–189). Yet schools often stress common content and skills that are deemed vital by Eurocentric standards at the cost of ignoring African identity and history, thereby denying African American children not only their history, but also their full humanity (Hilliard, 1995).

At its core, this form of schooling deprives African American children of knowledge of their history, examples of self-determination, and a cultural knowledge base that illuminates and reawakens their African mindedness (Hilliard, 1997). Those key experiences are known in hip-hop culture as Knowledge of Self, the fifth element of hip-hop. Because of the essential lessons it provides, the fifth element of hip-hop must be an essential component of hip-hop education. Foregrounding Knowledge of Self for hip-hop educators is a transformative practice that can begin to restore Black and Brown children's full humanity connected to deep learning experiences for their survival.

© KONINKLIJKE BRILL NV, LEIDEN, 2018 | DOI 10.1163/9789004371873_005

2   Moving toward Knowledge of Self & Critical Hip-hop Pedagogy

The above issues underline why, for me #HipHopEd's weekly discussion on February 5, 2013 was pivotal to shaping the field of Hip-hop Based Education (HHBE) as it focused on the fifth element of hip-hop. However, I want to contend that what hip-hop educators have normalized as HHBE cannot foster Knowledge of Self within our Black and Brown children. According to Irby and Hall (2011), HHBE typically refers to the use of rap songs and lyrics as pedagogical resources. Hill (2009) argues that hip-hop, and HHBE more broadly, has to be stretched beyond the meek appreciation of beats and rhymes to connect students' knowledge to their political and cultural identities. In my opinion, HHBE has fallen short by not integrating all the elements of hip-hop and by not basing the centrality of HHBE in the history and community of students. Emdin (2013) argues that the pillars of hip-hop culture are often ignored and prevent researchers, students, and teachers to move beyond superficialities with HHBE. Thus, I suggest we begin to look to a more radical HHBE, rooted in love, critical thinking, and social justice: Critical Hip-hop Pedagogy (CHHP).

In 2009, Akom introduced an alternative teaching method to HHBE that in my view pushed the field and ushered in a new pedagogical approach. This new method, CCHP, is deeply rooted to students' knowledge of self and their community with the goal of addressing social inequities. CCHP borrows from the work of critical race theorists to explore race and racism, oppression, experiential knowledge, and a commitment to social justice (Akom, 2009). Furthermore, CHHP is informed by Freire's notion of critical praxis. This teaching method is aimed exclusively at Black and Latina/o students in an effort to develop their critical thinking skills through the Freirian methodology of "problem posing," which consist of five stages: (1) identifying a problem, (2) analyzing a problem, (3) developing a plan, (4) implementing the plan, and (5) evaluating the plan (Akom, 2009; Gosa & Fields, 2012). The method allows children not only to learn not only their history, but also to think of ways to better their community through research that is rooted in "libertory principles of agency, equity, and self-determination" (Akom, p. 55). Lastly, CHHP emphasizes that "indigenous meaning and heritage are elevated as legitimate forms of knowledge" (Gosa & Fields, 2012, p. 197).

CHHP also embraces the established four primary elements of hip-hop – Graffiti (taggin'), MCing (rappin'/emceein'/spittin'), Dee-jaying, Breakdancing (B-boying and B-girling) – while stressing the fifth element. From hip-hop's conception, the production of knowledge has always been a central part of the culture and music, even as a youth movement built on fun, pleasure, and pain. The origins of hip-hop embraced empowering youth. In the borough of the Bronx, youth in the 1970s across the African diaspora pioneered a sound and culture rooted in African and African American traditions (Chang, 2005). However, Knowledge of Self functioned and still operates as the nexus for all elements derived from hip-hop culture, whether folks recognize it or not.

The five central elements constitute hip-hop as more than just a musical genre, but a site of social and cultural production with traditions, rituals, and customs that affirm youth identity on a global, national, and local level (Alim & Pennycook, 2007). Moreover, they illuminate a way of life for youth who engage with the culture. According to KRS-ONE (2004), "Rap is something you do, hip-hop is something you live" (p. 5). Therefore, when HHBE embraces only the element of rap, it is not engaging with the full culture of hip-hop. Furthermore, solely focusing on rap music ignores the rich and transformative power of hip-hop. Thus, students' exposure to HHBE is fragmented, much like their knowledge of what it means to be of African American or of African descent (Love, 2012).

Arguably, African American youth, by no fault of their own, have a limited understanding of African history and traditions, but at the end of the day they are still African. According to Diop (1981/1991), "[i]mperialism, like the prehistoric hunter, first killed the being spiritually and culturally, before trying to eliminate it physically" (p. 10). Diop adds that, "[t]he negation of the history and intellectual accomplishments of Black Africans was cultural, mental murder" (p. 10). Diop's premise can be utilized to explain why most youth have a tapered knowledge of hip-hop's history and traditions. Furthermore, most youth who engage with hip-hop music and culture only fully participate with one or two elements, but identify with hip-hop as their primary culture. However, most of these youth are unaware of hip-hop's intellectual and activist prowess, along with its history. Thus, there is dire need for CHHP because, in order to survive, Black and Brown children need an educational framework that address issues within their community while recognizing, affirming, and honoring African and African American history, traditions, and customs.

3   Knowledge of Self & Community

The fifth element of hip-hop is also incomplete without directly naming community. The creators of hip-hop understood the interconnectedness of their surroundings, the lived experiences of young people growing up in the Bronx and throughout New York City, the effects of postindustrial America, the impact of decaying public education, police brutality, poverty, racism, and the continual reinvention of the Black Arts Movement (1965–1975). At its core, each element of hip-hop arose from urban youths' Knowledge of Self and their understanding of their community. The cultural artifacts and traditions of hip-hop are products of the knowledge that urban youth constructed based on the social, political, economic and educational conditions of the 1970s and onward. According to Diaz (2010), youths' intrapersonal skills are illuminated "through the understanding of the fifth element, knowledge of self, and [their] interpersonal intelligence is shown through knowledge of the community as community organizer, teacher, and activist" (Diaz, 2010, p. 8). For example, one of the springboards for MCing was the critical conscious poetry of the Last Poets, namely Sonia Sonchez and Gil Scott-Heron. Moreover, the catalyst for MCing and B-girling/B-boying was a desire to articulate sonically, aesthetically, and kinesthetically, the day-to-day struggles of being marginalized and invisible in society. Young Black and Brown folks utilized the knowledge they gained from the African diaspora, urban streets, Black popular music, Jamaican dancehalls, and American society as a whole to form hip-hop culture. The culture and sound of hip-hop drew on musicality, sampling, dancing, language, entrepreneurship and urban visual arts to create Graffiti, MCing, Dee-jaying and Breakdancing (Chang, 2005; Rose, 1994). Therefore, Knowledge of Self is dependent on community. According to Richardson (2006), "one of the basic principles of hip-hop's ideology is to confront officially prescribed or received knowledge with local knowledge" (p. 43). Put another way, hip-hop's foundation is embedded in the act of critically reading one's reality – community – to understand oppression and domination to create counter narratives of love, pain, pleasure, and activism.

The transformative teaching approach of CHHP and Knowledge of Self intentionally addresses issues within students' communities aligned with the principles of social justice. Youth engaging in education that is driven by their experiences, constructing knowledge that is formed by their own ecosystem, is critical in helping students learn how to utilize their hip-hop identity to promote social change. It is for precisely that reason why in 2012, I created the hip-hop course, Real Talk: Hip-hop Education for Social Justice. The course is designed for elementary-aged students, a group often ignored within HHBE, to teach youth through the alternative teaching approach of CHHP.

4   Do Believe Me, Just Watch, Listen to Me!

> We keep pushing the narrative that education is a way out of the hood rather thana way to improve the hood. (Christopher Emdin, 2/13/2014, #HipHopEd)

The success of Real Talk has been well documented through instructional teaching videos. These videos can be found at bettinalove.com. However, I want to illustrate the power of CHHP and the fifth element linked to community through words of youth. In the 2012–2013 school year, 17 fifth graders were enrolled in Real Talk at a local elementary school in Atlanta, GA, The Kindezi School. The course taught students the history and five pillars of hip-hop, with special emphasis on the fifth element: Knowledge of Self and Community. When students were asked during their exit interviews, "We talk a lot of about knowledge of self and knowledge of community. What does that mean to you?" they responded in very similar ways:

> It means like your knowledge to yourself and don't give up on yourself. (Robert)

> Like know yourself and the community and...use that knowledge to make good decisions and help other people. (Kelly)

> It means to you know your community and to know yourself. What you can do and what you can't do. (Malcolm)

These student comments illustrate that centering Knowledge of Self and Community is vital to HHBE and making Emdin's words a reality. CCHP is way to help students improve their hood by gaining an understanding that one way to make changes in their community is to first recognize their own abilities to contribute to community building through their hip-hop identity – their culture. CHHP is not the only road to progressive hip-hop education that so many of us yearn for, but it's a concrete start. Finally, CHHP can be a springboard toward what Dr. Martin Luther King Jr. called a beloved community. One of the tenets of a beloved community is "[a]n understanding that 'whatever affects one directly affects all indirectly'" (King, 1963). Thus, if hip-hop education is the next movement, we need to sharpen our tools, build our collective, and center our work on the fifth element, Knowledge of Self and Community.

References

Akom, A. A. (2009). Critical hip-hop pedagogy as a form of liberatory praxis. *Equity & Excellence in Education, 42*(1), 52–66.

Alim, H. S., & Pennycook, A. (2007). Glocal linguistic flows: Hip-hop culture(s), identities, and the politics of language education. *Journal of Language, Identity, and Education, 6*(2), 89–100. doi:10.1080/15348450701341238

Brown, J. (2009). *Babylon girls: Black women performers and the shaping of the modern*. Durham, NC: Duke University Press.

Chang, J. (2005). *Can't stop won't stop: A history of the hip-hop generation*. New York, NY: St. Martin's Press.

Diop, C. A. (1991). *Civilization or barbarism: An authentic anthropology*. Chicago, IL: Chicago Review Press.

Emdin, C. (2013). Pursuing the pedagogical potential of the pillars of hip-hop through urban science education. *The International Journal of Critical Pedagogy, 4*(3), 83–97.

Gosa, L. T., & Fields, G. T. (2012). Is hip-hop education another hustle? The (ir)responsible use of hip-hop as pedagogy. In B. J. Porfilio & M. J. Viola (Eds.), *Hip-Hop(e): The Cultural Practice and Critical Pedagogy of International Hip-Hop* (pp. 1–24). New York, NY: Peter Lang.

Hill, M. L. (2009). *Beats, rhymes, and classroom life: Hip-hop pedagogy and the politics of identity*. New York, NY: Teachers College Press.

Hilliard, A. G. (1995). *The maroon within us: Selected essays on African American community socialization*. Baltimore, MD: Black Classic Press.

Hilliard, A. G. (1997). *SBA: The reawakening of the African mind*. Gainesville, FL: Makare Publishing.

Irby, D. J., & Hall, H. B. (2011). Fresh faces, new places: Moving beyond teacher-researcher perspectives in hip-hop-based education research. *Urban Education, 46*(2), 216–240. doi:0.1177/0042085910377513

King, M. L. (1963). *Why we can't wait*. New York, NY: Signet Classics.

KRS-One. (1989). You must learn (Artist by Boogie Down Productions). On *ghetto music: The blueprint of hip hop* [CD]. New York, NY: Jive Records.

Love, B. L. (2012). *Hip-hop's li'l sistas speak: Negotiating hip hop identities and politics in the new south*. New York, NY: Peter Lang.

Richardson, E. (2006). *Hip-hop literacies*. New York, NY: Routledge.

Rose, T. (1994). *Black noise: Rap music and Black culture in contemporary America*. Hanover, NH: Wesleyan University Press.

PART 2

Performance as Pedagogy

∵

Tweets

..

 Christopher Emdin
@ChrisEmdin

To be Hip-hop is to be scientific. To respond
to data/information, to be critical, to require
evidence, to analyze deeply #HipHopEd

 Edmund Adjapong Ph.D
@KingAdjapong

#ScienceGenius shows students that they
can be their authentic selves and identify as
scientists #HipHopEd

Amil Cook
@AmilCook

When our curriculum, instruction & content
is radical, rebellious and relevant students
of the HipHop Generation will "Go Hard"!
#HipHopEd

 Dr.JuNa
@DrJ512

Intersectionality is important. Let students
identify how issues impact their lives. Let
THEM name it. #activism #HipHopEd

E!
@etheemcee

Science Genius is an opportunity 2 tear
down stereotypes while using the 1 outlet
that the education system wouldn't, Hip
Hop! #HipHopEd

Introduction to Part 2: Performance as Pedagogy

Edmund Adjapong
@KingAdjapong

One of the most critical aspects of hip-hop is the art of performance. When engaging in any creative element of hip-hop culture the art of performance is at the core of how that creative element is presented or displayed. True participants of hip-hop culture understand the importance and tremendous amount of preparation that goes into any hip-hop performance. Hip-hop artists practice their elaborate concert sets for weeks on end before going on tour to ensure that participants of their shows have an unforgettable experience. B-boys/B-girls practice their intricate break dance moves before heading out to perform or battle a rival dance crew. Graffiti artists continuously practice drawing their elaborate visual art pieces on paper, consider and calculate the dimensions of the space where their visual art will live before creating vivid murals. Performance lies at the core of hip-hop, but participants of hip-hop are not the only individuals who engage in the art of performance. The art of performance can easily be transferred to the realities of teachers in any classroom space. In a study about the traits of effective educators, the act of performing is identified as a trait that many effective teachers possess (Polk, 2006). When teachers are in front of tens of gazing students, for up to ninety minutes at a time in many schools, it is necessary for them to find ways to engage, excite and empower students around content. Considering the act of teaching as a performance can be valuable to all educators because it encourages teachers to always prepare to be their best selves when they are in front of students. When educators consider teaching as the act of performance, ideally, they will practice their lessons before engaging students to ensure that there will be no gaps in instruction, that there are moments where they are captivating students and including students in the delivery of content and that there are moments of humor throughout the lesson. Considering the act of performance as pedagogy will encourage teachers to step out of their comfort zone and engage students in exciting and unforgettable lessons because have prepared and practiced their lessons extensively. When teachers view the act of performance as pedagogy, they are more inclined to be engaging to their students because they are always reflecting and perfecting their performance as an educator.

© KONINKLIJKE BRILL NV, LEIDEN, 2018 | DOI 10.1163/9789004371873_006

In this part, we interrogate the act of performance as pedagogy. In particular, we uncover the experiences of teachers and students who participated in the *Science Genius B.A.T.T.L.E.S. (Bringing Attention to Transforming Teaching and Learning in Science) Program*; an initiative focused on utilizing the power of hip-hop to engage urban youth who have been traditionally disengaged in science classrooms. The primary activity of the *Science Genius B.A.T.T.L.E.S.* program involves students creating science-themed raps or spoken word pieces based on science topics that they are learning in their science classrooms. The chapters in this part also interrogate the experiences of teachers who participated the *Science Genius B.A.T.T.L.E.S.* program who understood the importance of stepping out of their comfort zone as educators and perform to engage their students in science.

In the first chapter of this part, Edmund Adjapong provides an overview of the *Science Genius B.A.T.T.L.E.S.* program and discusses the multiple groups, including teachers and community members who are involved in ensuring students gain valuable experiences through the program. Adjapong further makes the argument for the necessity for innovative teaching practices and programs that are anchored in hip-hop culture to reach urban youth across all content areas, but most importantly in STEM (Science, Technology, Engineering & Mathematics). In the second chapter of this part, Tara Ware, a science educator in the Bronx, shares her experiences as an educator who initially did not identify as part of hip-hop culture, but teaches students who identify as a part of the hip-hop generation. Tara explains how connected students were to hip-hop culture and used that as an opportunity to utilize hip-hop as a tool to engage her students in her science classroom. She further shares how she had to step out of her comfort zone and look at pedagogy as performance for her students to truly buy into her using hip-hop as a pedagogical tool as an outsider of hip-hop culture. In the third chapter of this part, Tina Khan a science educator from Toronto shares her experiences as an educator pioneering the first effort to take the *Science Genius B.A.T.T.L.E.S.* program international and implement the program in schools outside of the United States. Finally, in the last chapter of this part, Elicia Estime shares her experiences as a student who participated in the *Science Genius B.A.T.T.L.E.S.* program. When implementing educational programs for youth, we rarely consider the experiences of the young people who we initially set out to support. In her chapter, Elicia shares how participating in the *Science Genius B.A.T.T.L.E.S.* program provided her an opportunity to view science in a positive light and allowed her to build positive relationships with adults who support her in all of her endeavors. In this part, you will find many stories representing the stakeholders and participants the *Science Genius B.A.T.T.L.E.S.* program.

Reference

Polk, J. A. (2006). Traits of effective teachers. *Arts Education Policy Review, 107*(4), 23–29.

CHAPTER 4

Toward the Development of *Science Geniuses*

Edmund Adjapong
@KingAdjapong

As schools are encouraged to move toward an approach to teaching and learning that is inclusive of 21st-century skills, collaboration, communication, critical thinking, and creativity, it is essential that they continue to work towards incorporating students' culture within school spaces (Rotherham & Willingham, 2010). There are many programs, mostly homegrown by teachers in their respective locales, that utilize hip-hop to engage youth in schools across. One of the most notable programs that utilizes hip-hop in schools is Flocabulary (Harrison & Rappaport, 2006). Flocabulary "is a library of songs, videos, and activities for K-12 online learning. Thousands of teachers use Flocabulary's educational raps and lesson plans to supplement their instruction and engage students" (Flocabulary Educational Hip-hop). While Flocabulary is often incorporated within the curriculum in many schools, most programs that utilize hip-hop to engage youth in educational spaces are forced to operate during "outside of school time," such as during lunch or after the school day. Many teachers who understand the power of using hip-hop as education in schools are forced to create opportunities to engage their students using hip-hop when school is over mostly because school administrators do not value hip-hop or see hip-hop as education and therefore are adamantly against incorporating it into the curricula. In other instances, teachers recognize the power of using hip-hop as education in schools, but have not received adequate training on how to utilize hip-hop as pedagogy. They are are unaware of how to incorporate hip-hop into their curriculum in an authentic fashion. Conversely, some educators do not understand or see the value of utilizing students' culture to engage them in content. It's important to note that a majority of teachers do not value students' culture in schools, especially hip-hop culture because many view hip-hop through their perception of rap music that is violent and misogynistic (Gay, 2002). I argue that hip-hop is a nuanced culture that has impacted and empowered youth populations from across the globe, especially youth of marginalized groups, since its conception (Adjapong & Emdin, 2015; Dunley, 2000) and rap, which is an integral part of hip-hop culture accounts for a small portion hip-hop's overall culture. Through understanding the power and potential

© KONINKLIJKE BRILL NV, LEIDEN, 2018 | DOI 10.1163/9789004371873_007

for hip-hop as education, in this chapter I explore the nuances and benefits of *Science Genius B.A.T.T.L.E.S.* (*Bringing Attention to Transforming Teaching and Learning in Science*) program, a hip-hop themed science program that serves as a hip-hop based intervention for youth who have traditionally been marginalized in youth in science classes during the school day through rap. The program involves writing and performing science-themed raps and engaging in a competition/battle to showcase students' science-themed raps.

1   **The Science Genius B.A.T.T.L.E.S. Program**

The *Science Genius B.A.T.T.L.E.S.* program is identified as a Hip-hop Based Intervention (HHBI), to increase urban students' affinity for science, that consists of a curriculum that can be incorporated into the high school science curriculum. The program introduces students to the wonders of science through hip-hop lyric writing and exploration of science content and is composed of multiple components to ensure it's seamless operation which includes, students, teachers, and community members. The primary activity of the *Science Genius B.A.T.T.L.E.S.* program is for participating students to craft science-themed raps or science spoken word poems using the science content that is being taught in their science class. When creating science-themed raps and science spoken word poems students are encouraged to make connections between their raps and their lived experiences. Throughout the program, students are also encouraged to continue perfecting their raps and poems even outside of the classroom as an extension of science learning. When students are encouraged and provided opportunities to make connections between science content and using familiar approaches of engagement (hip-hop) they are more likely to develop a deeper understanding of science content (Adjapong & Emdin, 2015; Adjapong, 2017). Students are provided multiple entry points to engage with science content, both through the traditional science curriculum and *Science Genius B.A.T.T.L.E.S.* program curriculum. At the end of each semester, students participate in a task that encourages them to perform their favorite science-themed rap or spoken word poem for their class. Performance as pedagogy benefits students in some ways as it provides opportunities for students to showcase their brilliance for their peers and teachers, which traditional science curriculum does not necessarily allow (Adjapong & Emdin, 2015). When students perform their science-themed raps, they become the masters of content knowledge because they gain a deep understanding of science content through science lyric writing. Throughout the program, students have an opportunity to battle (compete) one another as their peers and science teacher judges who has the best science-themed rap or spoken word poem to represent that class in future battles. Students within each class battle one another until there is one winner per class. Then, student finalists from each class battle one another until there is one finalist per school. Finally, each Science Genius winner from each school participates in a culminating Science Genius Final Battle, where only one Science Genius is crowned and dubbed the Science Genius of the year.

The Science Genius Battle is held within the community, at a local university or performance space such as a theater or community center to expose students to spaces that they would not normally have access to. But more importantly, for students who are performing their science-themed raps to feel like celebrities as they demonstrate their science content knowledge on a grand stage in front of an audience of their peers, family members, and community members. During the Science Genius Final Battles, student performances and science-themed raps/spoken word poems assessed by the judges who are scientists, hip-hop artist, and school leaders. To date, over two-thousand students have participated in the Science Genius Program from across the country and international cities that include Toronto, Quebec, Calgary, Alberta and Kingston, Jamaica.

2   The Necessity for a Science Hip-hop Based Intervention: The Science Genius Program

The *Science Genius B.A.T.T.L.E.S.* program was intentionally designed to increase engagement amongst urban youth who have historically been marginalized in schools (Wald & Losen, 2003). Researchers and educators have noted a significant lack of engagement and what can be described as an aversion for learning in schools. This is specifically true for Black and Latino/a students in science classrooms, even when the reason for their disengagement and aversion is out of their control. There are many reasons why students of color may not be interested in science including "envision[ing] the field of science as distant and inaccessible" (Basu & Barton, 2007, p. 467), or the lack the resources and equipment necessary in K-12 settings to provide them with authentic science experiences. According to Munce and Fraser (2012) African-American students' interest in STEM has decreased significantly over time, is now lower than that of any other ethnic group, and is expected to remain low in the years to come. Additionally, there is an achievement gap in science that exists between African-American/Latino/a urban students and their counterparts from other ethnic and less diverse social settings. According to the National Center for Education Statistics (2015), amongst 4th graders nationwide there is 14% gap of achievement in science between

Black students as compared to their White counterparts, which increases to 17.4% when comparing Black and White students in the eighth grade. The National Center for Education Statistics (2015) reported a similar trend when considering the achievement in science between Latinx students and White students, reporting a gap of achievement of 12.5% amongst fourth-grade students and a gap of 13.9% amongst 8th-grade students. When identifying gaps of achievement amongst groups of students who have historically been socially marginalized, it's particularly important that we consider incorporating youth culture, such as hip-hop, into the science curriculum to engage students in science through a means in which they see themselves in the content and pedagogy. Unfortunately, there continues to be an ongoing misunderstanding of the experiences and realities of African-American and Latino/a students who predominantly populate urban settings (Kahle, Meece, & Scantlebury, 2000; Seiler, 2001). In order to gain insight into urban students' experiences, I argue that education researchers develop and suggest innovative approaches that "focus explicitly on understanding the realities of youth within urban classrooms and supports the teacher in utilizing an understanding of these realities as an anchor for instruction delivery" (Emdin, 2011, p. 5).

3   Teachers at the Frontlines of Science Genius

Teachers play a critical role in *Science Genius B.A.T.T.L.E.S.* program as they are on the front lines of implementing this HHBI in the science classroom. Through professional development teachers are provided an opportunity learn the theory, practices, and curriculum of the *Science Genius B.A.T.T.L.E.S.* program. With a majority of teachers identifying as White and and an outsider of urban communities and hip-hop culture, it's important to prepare teachers to engage in any HHBI. Similar to students, teachers are pushed out of their comfort zones when implementing *Science Genius B.A.T.T.L.E.S.* program in their classrooms, especially if they do not have a direct connection to hip-hop culture. The beauty of the *Science Genius B.A.T.T.L.E.S.* program is that through utilizing hip-hop and making connections to science content students who identify as hip-hop have opportunities to teach their teachers about hip-hop and teachers who are experts in science content to have opportunities to engage their students in science utilizing their students' culture. Both teachers and students are able to develop more positive relationships that are anchored and facilitated by hip-hop culture, and teachers can gain authentic understandings of youth culture while building positive and sustainable relationships with students.

4   Science Genius B.A.T.T.L.E.S. and the Community

Another essential component of the *Science Genius B.A.T.T.L.E.S.* program
is the support of the local community at large. While the Science Genius
Program is incorporated within the existing curriculum of any science class,
the program is supported by volunteer community members who volunteer
to dedicate their time and talent to work with students to increase student
engagement in science. During the *Science Genius B.A.T.T.L.E.S.* program,
hip-hop ambassadors are recruited from the community to support
teachers in their implementation of the program. Hip-hop ambassadors
are individuals who are local hip-hop artist and have the ability to work
with teachers on the authentic execution of the program and students
on their lyric writing development. The hip-hop ambassadors are often
individuals who themselves have had negative experiences in schools
and been pushed out of schools, but believe in the power of hip-hop as
education and therefore are committed to supporting teachers and youth
who are currently in schools have a better experience than they did while
participating in this HHBI.

    In addition to hip-hop ambassadors, the entire local community is involved
in the *Science Genius B.A.T.T.L.E.S.* program. The *Science Genius* Final Battles is
a culminating event that occurs at the conclusion of the program and is open
to the community to attend. At the *Science Genius* Final Battles students from
each participating school perform their science-themed raps with emotion and
pride in front of an audience of hundreds of community members showcasing
their brilliance. Community members file through the rows of theaters to
see and cheer for youth as they showcase their science content knowledge
through an authentic cultural art form. In turn, community members are
susceptible to learning science content through students' performance of
their science-themed raps/spoken word poems. In many cases, community
members are inspired by student science performances. Students from each
of the participating schools attend the Final Battles in large numbers cheering
their school's *Science Genius* on and participating teachers are present
reciting students rhymes that they have repeatedly checked for the accuracy
of science content. The entire community is involved in the implementation
of the *Science Genius B.A.T.T.L.E.S.* program. It is important for families to
have access to schools, but it is even more important to dismantle traditional
school policies that invite parents to schools for conferences to invite them to
school for students for a showcase of students' science brilliance. Through the
participation of the community, the *Science Genius B.A.T.T.L.E.S.* program filled
with a substantial amount of positive energy that is anchored in science and
hip-hop as education.

5   Toward the Development of Science Geniuses

Through engaging in the *Science Genius B.A.T.T.L.E.S.* program students
are provided a space to explore their own emotional experiences and make
connections between their lived experiences and science content. Students
have used their science-themed raps as an outlet to express emotions that
they carry with themselves every day, which included anger and frustration.
But by having the space to disclose emotional experience, students are
afforded the opportunity to merge the science content that they learned in
the classroom with their emotional experiences. Through creating science-
themed raps, students are also able to reflect and make connections between
their multiple identities, including their science/academic identity and hip-
hop identity. One *Science Genius* winner used her science-themed rap as a
platform to discuss her frustrations about the lack of women represented in
the sciences and her ability to be successful in STEM, while still describing
cell theory. Another Science Genius winner wrote a science-themed rap about
navigating challenging obstacles in his community, making and learning from
his mistakes but still motivated to work hard to reach his academic goals while
making connections to Newton's laws of motion.

Through participating in the *Science Genius B.A.T.T.L.E.S* program as
a HHBI, students are in a position to acquire science content knowledge
through non-traditional practices. Students shared on numerous accounts
that they were able to use their reflections on their science-theme raps to
support them while taking state exams necessary for graduation. Participating
this the Science Genius Program provided an opportunity for students to
feel like celebrities and gain praise similar to that of a local celebrity, but for
their persistence in science. Interestingly, when these students used science-
themed raps to explore emotional content, they were each able to come to new
conclusions regarding their identity.

The criticisms targeted at hip-hop and its supposed propensity for violence,
misogyny, and materialism are valid to an extent. But these perceptions of the
culture are guided by corporate media-driven narratives that highlight a thin
slice of a robust culture and makes the most problematic aspects of the culture
hyper-visible (Emdin, 2010). The effort to use hip-hop as a tool for engaging
students in science and performance also challenges negative stereotypes of
hip-hop culture and is a step in the right direction for hip-hop as education
being validated in schools across the country. Utilizing HHBI in the classroom
provides new possibilities for educators who wish to engage students using
youth culture. It also provides educators with an approach to connect science
content to one of the students' multiple identities, which leads to students
gaining a stronger connection between self and the content. The Science

Genius Program also allows teachers and stakeholders of education witness the power of hip-hop culture as education.

References

Adjapong, E. S., & Emdin, C. (2015). Rethinking pedagogy in urban spaces: Implementing hip-hop pedagogy in the urban science classroom. *Journal of Urban Learning, Teaching, and Research, 11*, 66–77.

Basu, S. J., & Barton, A. C. (2007). Developing a sustained interest in science among urban minority youth. *Journal of Research in Science Teaching, 44*(3), 466–489.

Dunley, T. (2000, May 12). The colour barrier is no more: So whose music is it anyway? *Montreal Gazette*, p. A1.

Emdin, C. (2010). Affiliation and alienation: Hip-hop, rap, and urban science education. *Journal of Curriculum Studies, 42*(1), 1–25.

Emdin, C. (2011). Moving beyond the boat without a paddle: Reality pedagogy, Black youth, and urban science education. *The Journal of Negro Education, 80*(3), 284–295.

Flocabulary Educational Hip-hop. (n.d.). Retrieved December 17, 2017, from https://www.flocabulary.com/

Gay, G. (2002). Preparing for culturally responsive teaching. *Journal of Teacher Education, 53*(2), 106–116.

Harrison, B., & Rappaport, A. (2006). *Flocabulary: The hip-hop approach to SAT-level vocabulary building*. Kennebunkport, ME: Cider Mill Press.

Kahle, J. B., Meece, J., & Scantlebury, K. (2000). Urban African-American middle school science students: Does standards-based teaching make a difference? *Journal of Research in Science Teaching, 37*(9), 1019–1041.

Munce, R., & Fraser, E. (2012). *Where are the STEM students? What are their career interests*. Retrieved from https://www.stemconnector.org/sites/default/files/store/STEM-Students-STEM-Jobs-Executive.Summary.pdf

National Center for Education Statistics. (2015). *The nation's report card: Science 2015*. Washington, DC: Institute of Education Sciences and U.S. Department of Education.

Rotherham, A. J., & Willingham, D. T. (2010). "21st-century" skills. *American Educator, 34*, 17–20.

Seiler, G. (2001). Reversing the "standard" direction: Science emerging from the lives of African American students. *Journal of Research in Science Teaching, 38*(9), 1000–1014.

Wald, J., & Losen, D. J. (2003). Defining and redirecting a school-to-prison pipeline. *New Directions for Student Leadership, 2003*(99), 9–15.

CHAPTER 5

Learning alongside My Students through the *Science Genius B.A.T.T.L.E.S.* Program

Tara Ware
@Twareo505

I am a science educator. I am a New York City public school teacher. My students come from various backgrounds and readiness levels. Over the last eight years, I have experimented using multiple projects and teaching approaches to engage my students in increasing their science content knowledge while gaining deeper connections with the content. In my search for the most efficient teaching devices one of the most well-known songs in the English-speaking world popped into my head:

> ABCDEFG...HIJK-LMNOP...QRS...TUV...WX...Y AND Z...now I know my ABCs, next time won't you sing with me!

As experienced through the alphabet song, music and rhythm is obviously an amazing way to engage students in curriculum and assist them with memorization. I believe songs, rap, poems, rhymes, etc., are fantastic tools to help students, because not only are they catchy, but they also significantly increase student participation in the classroom and with the content.

So the more specific question becomes: Why hip-hop? I have incorporated hip-hop into all of my science Regents classes during the past six years, and I have seen steady increases in regents passing rates and overall student learning. Put rhythmically into one of the science-themed rhymes that I used to model for my students:

> *Hip-hop taps into student success/*
> *It helps my students do their best/*
> *It helps them all to pass their tests/*
> *And below is why – hip-hop is progress!*

1   Hip-hop Is Culture

One of the most memorable times that I spent with my students was at the *Science Genius* Final Battles. They would practice and perform for the show weeks in advance and state, "Miss Ware, I feel famous on stage." I would see them in the halls, during lunch, and in the staircases practicing, editing, and perfecting their raps. The salutatorian, Judith Nkwor, of our school summed it best when she stated in her graduation speech:

> *Watching you, my classmates, reminded me of something that Ms. Ware said in tenth grade. I believe she said to me, "Why are you so shy? You have one of the most supportive classes." We were to create a rap about an Earth Science topic and to perform it in front of our class. I was hesitant about going up. But after Ms. Ware said those words, everyone started cheering for me, "Go Juju!" "Go Juju," and they gave me the confidence to do it. They sang along with me and clapped for me through the whole thing. That was when I came to value the group of people that I am honored to call my classmates. Your encouragement, kindness, and compassion, is what differentiates you from others. Though there were times when we argued and fought, it could never compare to the times where we laughed, played, and uplift each other. Those are the moments that I will cherish the most.*

The young lady emphasized in her speech how performing her science-themed rap in front of her peers, and then watching her peers perform, made her feel like she belonged and was part of a broader community and family. From my firsthand observations, and from the feedback from my students, I firmly believe that participation in the *Science Genius B.A.T.T.L.E.S.* (*Bringing Attention to Transforming Teaching and Learning in Science*) program brought my students together. Encouraging students to write science-themed raps allowed them to bond through the creation and sculpting of lyrics that demonstrated their content knowledge and connections to their lives and the rap performances which facilitated a supportive environment for creativity and expression. There's a specific type of feeling and belonging you get when you rap, sing or dance in front of a group of supportive students. The self-consciousness, timidness, and negative demeanors all disappear! It becomes an inclusive culture where everyone including myself as, an outsider of the culture, gets out of their shells. It also allows students to express their multiple identities including their hip-hop identity, which oftentimes isn't encouraged in schools. It truly is an amazing phenomenon when everyone cheers each other on and laughs as they create science-themed raps. I remember when I first decided to rap in front of my students to show students that I can step outside of my comfort zone and participate in their culture. I was embarrassed, I was shy, but after that experience, we were all laughing and cheering. It changes the energy in the classroom, it contributes to the culture, and it allows students to bring their hip-hop identity into the science classroom.

2   Hip-hop Creates Engagement

I play music in my class; the students seem to get super excited. As soon as I play a popular hip-hop song, all students immediately begin to sing and engage. As soon as I play a science-themed rap, they are all listening and engaged, trying to figure out if they understand the science content within the song. Put simply, hip-hop in a classroom creates engagement because hip-hop is so ingrained in most of my students' lives and cultures. If they are able to pick their own beat, to their favorite song, then they can have fun while they learn. They can create a dance to their song, or just joke around while trying to determine what the next line should be. When I bring hip-hop into my classroom, I provide an opportunity for my students to be themselves. I usually have a 20% homework completion rate, but the percentage increases significantly when the final project is a science-themed rap. My students enjoy creating their science-themed raps and adding a beat behind the lyrics, and the increasing length of their songs challenges them to continue editing their science-themed raps, which leads to a deeper understanding of science content.

3   Hip-hop Creates Problem Solvers

Have you ever tried to do something you're not good at? Tried to build a robot? Tried to finish the Rubik's cube? Tried to write a rap? Well, I am not naturally talented at writing and memorizing lyrics to a hip-hop song. As a science educator, I know my science content, but I did not know how to put it in a smooth flowing rap. So how did I overcome this? I looked at raps and noticed how many syllables are in each line. I tried to fill them with content lyrics and storylines that brought the science content alive. I then practiced and practiced...and practiced some more until my lyrics had a beat to them. I then edited the lyrics and practiced again. This whole process was harder than writing a graduate school paper! It was something I was not used to, something I had to edit and revise and practice to feel confident. It was challenging, and since I knew the content, I learned how to problem solve. I learned how to create my science-themed rap through continuously work through it. Now, some of my students are just like me, they like to listen to rap, but they don't know how to rap. Therefore, the *Science Genius B.A.T.T.L.E.S.* does not only helps students understand science vocabulary and science content knowledge, but it also creates problem solvers. The process itself is difficult for the students (in uniquely different ways), and I can honestly see them struggling through it, but then getting so excited when they find that perfect rhyme and make connections between science and their lives. At that moment, they don't even know it, but they are problem solvers!

4   Hip-hop Creates Scientists

In my school, when I announced that we were going to create science-themed raps for the *Science Genius B.A.T.T.L.E.S.* program, immediately most of my students were interested. When we started practicing, I started losing some students' motivation because they realized how challenging creating lyrics around science content was, but their peers walked them through it. The real watershed moment for this program was when my students who were failing my class, who hated science, who were unmotivated, decided to put a lot of time and effort into these science-themed raps because they saw it as fun instead of "work." Little did they know, they were practicing and performing and dedicating so much time to crafting their rhymes and therefore learning science content. But it wasn't the prototypical work (the paper or worksheet), so they didn't complain and got it done with enthusiasm. Through the creation of science-theme raps, they were becoming actual scientists without even realizing it!

5   Hip-hop Creates Interest

I presented about raps to a group of teachers in Atlanta during the expeditionary learning school conference. I had two students Skype in, and one teacher from the audience asked "well if every class starts writing science-themed raps then won't it get too redundant, won't you be like, ugh, another rap?" and the kid responded "you guys give us papers in every class so why not a rap in every class?" The teachers laughed because they knew it was true. We give papers and tests as an assessment, so why not science-themed raps? Allowing students to create these science-themed raps gives students the opportunity to show that they are scientists in a different way. Students can create a rap on experimentation. They can create a rap on the plate tectonic cycle that relates to a love story in their life. Science becomes real for them and exciting. Raps take kids, who ordinarily weren't that interested in science, and make them dig deep, research science concepts so they would have more to rap about, read more from the textbooks so they can compete for that next best "bar."

6   Hip-hop Creates Performers/Presenters

One of the most challenging aspects of the *Science Genius B.A.T.T.L.E.S.* program was getting a shy student to perform theirs in front of the class. Once he or she does, he or she will always remember it. This past year a shy girl named Simone was in my class. She rarely volunteered and seemed to struggle with understanding many science concepts. She then wrote an amazing science-themed rap; I was so proud of her. But then when she presented it to the class, I was speechless. Her performance was amazing! She then worked for weeks to change a few lines and added additional science content to increase the rigor of her rap. When she went onto stage during the schools' *Science Genius* Battle, she immediately started to cry. She said she couldn't do it. Some of her friends ran onto the stage to support her and Simone gained the courage to perform her science-themed rap and rocked the show. These are the moments that the students will always remember, pushing through challenging times and experiences and ending up conquering fears and insecurities. It remarkable when a student gains the confidence to present in front of hundreds of people with confidence and pride and fluidity. She went from a shy girl to a great performer, and I will always be proud of her.

7   Hip-hop Creates Relationships

The *Science Genius B.A.T.T.L.E.S.* program has also served as the conduit to building significant relationships between the students themselves and between the students and teachers. During the school year, teachers listen to students' science-themed raps, we watch the videos that they create of their raps, and we read and give feedback on their science-themed raps to ensure the science content is accurate. The process is long and detailed. Therefore, when they get on stage during the Science Genius Final Battles, I feel like I'm their second mom. I feel like my child is going onto the stage and shining. I get a sense of pride, and their peers do too. When on stage performing their science-themed rap, students give their teachers shout outs, their parents are hugging them and taking pictures, and they have so much excitement from the work they put in throughout the year. It brings the entire community together. The *Science Genius B.A.T.T.L.E.S.* program shows how hard work can make anything possible. It's these moments that let you see more of the students' personalities and life stories beyond the textbooks and final exams.

8   Hip-hop Creates Academic Success

I believe that the *Science Genius B.A.T.T.L.E.S.* program has directly helped students to improve their test scores and has increased students' desire to learn and stay in school. Since the start of the rap program, my NYS Regents passage rates have increased each year, from 30% to almost 60% this year. I also believe that the supportive environment facilitated by the *Science Genius B.A.T.T.L.E.S.* program has helped students to form strong and supportive friendships that have helped promote positive behaviors. Additionally, for many of my students, rap has been that spark to wanting to learn even more about science. Overall, rap builds confidence, it stimulates creativity, it encourages students to have fun while learning, it creates friendships through a supportive community, and it is extremely effective at improving both participation and knowledge within the classroom.

CHAPTER 6

The Science Genius B.A.T.T.L.E.S.: The Toronto Experience

Tina Khan
@Mizzteacha

We entered the social media world of Twitter in 2011 and came across the weekly #HipHopEd conversations and the account of Dr. Chris Emdin. He was doing phenomenal work with urban youth and talking about a pedagogy that resonated with the practice of our program, Each1 Teach1. We began following his work and discovered that he was running a unique program called the *Science Genius B.A.T.T.L.E.S.* (*Bringing Attention to Transforming, Teaching and Learning Science*) program. the *Science Genius B.A.T.T.L.E.S.* is intended for students to increase engagement in science and improve their scientific literacy by writing and performing science-themed raps.

We immediately loved *Science Genius*; it challenged the framework that science learning could only be done by traditional methods such as labs and tests, while also bringing in an aspect of fun, excitement, and culture for youth. When we saw the video of the competition, we witnessed the students blossom when their brilliance was recognized and applied in the school setting. The *Science Genius B.A.T.T.L.E.S.* combined hip-hop, which many view as recreational or only a genre of music, and used it to create a learning opportunity in science. Science is perceived as an elitist discipline, one exclusively for White men or for those who are "smart enough." When "smart enough" is standard based on a system laden with systemic issues, it shuts out many urban youth. These youth are not seen as potential scientists. Using hip-hop allows us to break through that barrier for these students so that they can explore and demonstrate their scientific ability.

Although we really loved the idea of the *Science Genius B.A.T.T.L.E.S.* program, we didn't consider organizing a board-wide event until years later when we were strongly encouraged us to try it out in Toronto. Our city was an obvious choice to launch the *Science Genius B.A.T.T.L.E.S.*, we have been gaining international acclaim for our growing hip-hop industry, our most popular export being Drake who has affectionately renamed the city "The 6ix" in reference to our area code. However, we were still a little intimidated to run the *Science Genius B.A.T.T.L.E.S.* program in Toronto for many reasons. Although

© KONINKLIJKE BRILL NV, LEIDEN, 2018 | DOI 10.1163/9789004371873_009

our city is very cosmopolitan, we don't have the same public understanding and regard for hip-hop that New York City does, and we didn't think we would have the same level of interest in our schools. After all, New York City is the birthplace of hip-hop, everyone in that city seems to have a general knowledge about hip-hop culture, and the schools would have an easier time "selling" the idea of *Science Genius* to students. Would Toronto teachers and students be able to grasp the concept and produce quality work that would be on par with the excellence of the New York students? Our diversity of students didn't necessarily have the same exposure to hip-hop, and a lot of our Toronto schools have very high English Language Learners populations, would they be able to produce a science-themed rap song? There was only one way to find out, and that was to try!

Where does one begin when trying to launch a board-wide the *Science Genius B.A.T.T.L.E.S.* event? The first thing we did was network and build our team of educators who could support the *Science Genius B.A.T.T.L.E.S.* program with knowledge, resources, and funding. We sat down with multiple educators and brainstormed the idea of having the competition in Toronto. We thought about the following questions:

— What resources would we need and who could fund us?
— How would the event look? Would it be a school show or evening event?
— Who could participate? Would juniors and seniors compete together?
— How would we explain the *Science Genius B.A.T.T.L.E.S.* to all of the teachers in our school board?
— How would we be able to teach rap writing to both the teachers and students?
— What would our timeline be and how would we guide the teachers and students through the process?

Let's begin with our initial team. The Eachı Teachı Partnership is run by Suzaana Shebib and myself. We are both math and science teachers, between the both of us we have over 25 years teaching experience. We were both teaching science classes and could run pilot *Science Genius* lessons in our classes. It would also be interesting to juxtapose our hip-hop knowledge. My background in hip-hop was very limited, I love the culture, but for the most part, I only knew the older or mainstream music. I have since taken a university course to grow my understanding of hip-hop history and culture since I wouldn't call hip-hop my personal, cultural experience. Over the past few years, I have made a conscious effort to learn about the five elements of hip-hop and to understand the interests of my students by observing and talking with them to see what kinds of hip-hop they were consuming, mainly through social media platforms like YouTube, Instagram, and Twitter. Suzanna, on the other hand, was very embedded in hip-hop culture. She had grown up in it and was very familiar with the history, culture and even founding Toronto artists. Suzanna was a special education student as a child, and had experienced first hand what it was like to have teachers tell you "you can't," "you aren't smart enough" etc. As an educator, Suzanna has always wanted to increase the scientific literacy of the general public by making science more accessible. Together we work well as a team because we complement what the other needs and are not judgmental, we acknowledge that everyone has strengths to share and we build on that philosophy.

This brings me to the next member of our team Karen; she was one of our school board's science instructional leaders. Karen had no clue about hip-hop music or culture and no interest in it. However, she was 100% committed to engaging our urban youth, and that was all we hoped for. Karen had access to the list of schools and science department contacts, and through her, we could contact all of the teachers on the board. Initially, we suggested that she invite schools to participate in the *Science Genius B.A.T.T.L.E.S.* program. Furthermore, we asked her to advocate for the program and get us some funding from the Science Department at the Board level, which she obtained for us.

The last member of our team was Chelsea, she was a Student Equity worker, and she had access to the Equity Department staff. She communicated our needs to the department and was able to secure funding for things like bus tickets, food, and awards for the *Science Genius B.A.T.T.L.E.S.* events. She also attended the events and provided teacher coverage.

The next thing we did was set up an introductory package for the teachers explaining the ideas and theory of the *Science Genius B.A.T.T.L.E.S.* program. Our goal was to encourage each school to send a school finalist (either an individual or group) to our first Toronto *Science Genius B.A.T.T.L.E.S.* competition. We explained to the teachers how The Science Genius was a valuable learning experience for kids, particularly marginalized youth who did not traditionally do well with test-based evaluations. The *Science Genius B.A.T.T.L.E.S.* program provided a differentiated activity that could be offered to the diversity of learners that are overlooked in science classes such as our audio or musical intelligence.

We also provided a curriculum that detailed how to run and implement the *Science Genius B.A.T.T.L.E.S.* program within the traditional science curriculum. This included resources for teachers, classroom ideas and content examples; our focus was on minimizing the additional workload for the teacher. Many, teachers are not involved in hip-hop culture, and therefore potentially see this as intimidating. We tried to take the "scary part" out, and we even addressed some of the more controversial aspects of hip-hop and how to also address those in class.

We have 94 secondary schools in the Toronto School Board, and each school has its own unique culture. Therefore, we gave teachers many options for how they could participate in the *Science Genius B.A.T.T.L.E.S.* pilot.

1 They could run the *Science Genius B.A.T.T.L.E.S.* as an extracurricular club with their students.
2 They could use the *Science Genius B.A.T.T.L.E.S.* in their class. Students could write a science rap as an evaluated assignment or replace a culminating project. We created a lesson plan for writing science raps and provided a scoring rubric. We decided that it was not fair to evaluate students on their rapping skills, the scoring rubric did not include performance in the criteria.

We acknowledged that some science teachers would be reluctant to participate in the *Science Genius B.A.T.T.L.E.S.* program because they felt that they did not know enough about hip-hop to be able to engage their kids. To address this valid concern, we offered a one day workshop for students and teachers called Spit Camp, where professional hip-hop artists would teach students about writing and performing a rap. We extended this workshop to all the students so they would have access to the same training and mentorship. We provided the Spit Camp two weeks before schools had to declare their participation in the B.A.T.T.L.E.S. competition; we assumed this would give students and teachers an open window to assess how they would like to participate in the program. Through the course of the program, teachers began to realize that their knowledge of rapping was not a necessity to run the *Science Genius B.A.T.T.L.E.S.*, only their willingness to accommodate youth culture in their traditional learning spaces.

We invited teachers who were interested in participating in the *Science Genius B.A.T.T.L.E.S.* to attend an after-school information session. The team had planned to go over the program and lesson plan with the teachers, and offer suggestions how each school could run the program and select their school finalist. We were expecting a flood of RSVP emails to our information session and wanting to participate in the *Science Genius B.A.T.T.L.E.S.* program, after all, it was a pedagogically innovative program, it made teaching science literacy fun, and we were living in "the 6ix"!!! This was bound to be a hit! However, on the day of the session, we only got one teacher to attend. ONE! This did not discourage us, we went through with the session as planned and help our single attendee map out how she could run a the *Science Genius B.A.T.T.L.E.S.* curriculum for her school's entire grade 10 science cohort. She left the session very excited and we were also happy to have met her. Now, we just needed a few more schools to sign on, we estimated that 10 schools would be a good number to participate in the program.

1   **Spit Camp**

The Spit Camp was held as a one-day event with two workshops. We hired two Toronto hip-hop artists that we had worked with before; we were confident that these artists would be able to work with our students. Not everyone was made to teach, and it takes certain patience and understanding to encourage rambunctious youth to settle down to work on a task. We highly recommend that you hire artists that have previous experience with teaching youth. The science teachers from each school were also in attendance, along with our school board's science instructional leaders, to lend support to STEM aspects of the workshop.

The first workshop was called Writing Rhymes 101; the idea was to introduce the basics of writing a rhyming poem, it was run by a well known female Toronto hip-hop educator and MC named Motion. The first thing kids had to do was get a quick lesson about the four elements of hip-hop and the importance of the MC to hip-hop culture. Next students had to come up with their own MC name. Motion asked the kids two questions:

1   What tools did hip-hop artists need? *i.e., mixer, speakers, microphone, lights.*
2   What science did they see in those tools? *i.e., electricity, physics, energy.*

To get the students started on working on their science-themed rhymes, Motion put the answers from students questions on the board. We also provided the kids a science vocabulary bank with the scientific terminology that they had learned in their classes, being mindful to give grade specific vocabulary lists to each student. A motion then introduced the general scheme for writing a rap. Write two sentences, the last word in each sentence should rhyme with the other. For example:

> *Today we are going to write a science rap;*
> *None of that boring ish, tests only crap.*

The next progression was for the kids to write two sentences that rhyme, but using words from the board or the vocabulary sheet. After the kids had their two sentences, they got into a circle to form a cypher and share their bars. It was a lot of fun, and kids got to see that writing a rap was not a difficult as it once may have seemed, they had 2 bars in their hand, another 14 lines and they would have the traditional 16 bars of a hip-hop song.

Our second workshop was run by another well known Toronto producer and MC, Rich Kidd; it was called Punchlines and Performances. Rich began this workshop explaining metaphors to students in the class who were not sure what they were:

> A metaphor *is a figure of speech that refers to something as being the same as another thing for rhetorical effect. It may provide clarity or identify hidden similarities between two ideas.*

He moved into talking about the concept of the "punchline" in hip-hop songs, lyrically clever use of a work or a catchy phrase or quote. The punchline is intended to grab the audience's attention and make them react. We put up some punchlines and let the students decide if it was a punchline and why. Make sure you select "PG" punchlines for your younger audience. You can also use this opportunity to talk about profane language in hip-hop if you wish. Educators and parents have a reasonable concern that hip-hop uses some explicit language and they do not want this being celebrated or reproduced by their kids. Although we didn't want to censor our students, we wanted the song to be played for a public audience, so we told the kids that they had to produce a "clean version" or "radio edit" of their song if they wanted to include words that were not appropriate for a school setting.

Below are some metaphors we used. Metaphors are a fixture in hip-hop music, and you can almost find them in any song. If you wish, you can even make a side assignment with hip-hop and metaphors, having kids find their metaphors or punchlines in songs.

"Her feet hurt, I call it shoe-icide" – Fabulous, You be killin' em'
**shoe-icide/suicide

"young ni***s that blast-for-me, no religion" – Jay-Z, Dear Summer
** "blast-for-me"/"blasphemy"

"Why I'm watching every n**** watching me closely?
My s*** is butter for the bread, they wanna toast me" – Jay Z, Can I live.

"I keep my twisted grill, just to show the kids it's real,
we ain't picture perfect but we worth the picture still" – J.Cole, Crooked Smile

"Everybody gon' respect the shooter
But the one in front of the gun lives forever" – Kendrick Lamar, Money Trees

"You love her, then you gotta give the world to her
Is that a world tour or your girl's tour?
I know that you gotta be a thug for her
This ain't what she meant when she told you to open up more." – Drake,
Back to Back.

The exit activity in this workshop was for kids to write 4 bars including one punchline, and then share their work with the class. We used a simple rhyming scheme for the kids:

1   sentence ends with word A
2   sentence ends with word that rhymes with A
3   sentence ends with work B
4   sentence ends with a word that rhymes with B

Some kids got into it and wrote full songs, and others just wrote the 4 bars. Some students were shy to perform and they were allowed to either have the instructors read out their work or simply pass. However, even the shy ones seemed to draw some courage at the end of the session and share their work, it was amazing to see their confidence soar!

Rich closed out the session with giving some performance techniques and letting kids think about how they were going to add their own swagger or personality into their work. Artists always have a little performance characteristic that is unique to them, it can be hand gestures, a little dance, they way they rock the mic, their outfits, etc... It was good food for thought for our budding artists.

2   The Science Genius B.A.T.T.L.E.S.

We planned for the schools to have almost a month and a half to work with their students and select their school finalist. We let each school decide how they would set up their school selection process. One of the schools that participated was located in a middle-class neighborhood; it was reputed to be a highly academic school and most of the children where from immigrant households. It was not the typical urban school we had envisioned to participate in the program. The teacher ran the *Science Genius B.A.T.T.L.E.S.* program as a culminating assignment for her Grade 11 Biology class, and she was blown away by the work the students produced. She said she had never seen her students so enthusiastic about an assignment and they had set aside a "Rap Day" for everyone to perform their raps. She said it was her favorite day of teaching and she would run the program again.

To prepare for the event, we chose a school that was in a convenient location. We contacted the school A.V. department to make sure they could provide the necessary equipment (microphones, projector, etc.) and we ran a rehearsal with every finalist's background music to make sure everything would go smoothly on the day of the event. We also printed out a certificate of participation and brought medals for everyone; we wanted every student who went on stage to feel like a winner for having the courage to try something new. For the top two finalists in the *Science Genius B.A.T.T.L.E.S.*, we bought a trophy so that they would feel appreciated for winning. Finally, we asked hip-hop artists and STEM professionals to volunteer to judge the competition.

The day of the competition was buzzing with excitement! The students were very supportive of each performance; the junior students were surprisingly more competitive than we had thought. Our 3rd place winner was a grade 8 female who rapped about fluids, and it was great to see a girl breaking the gender stereotype that an MC could only be a male. The 2nd place winner was a grade 11 male who rapped about energy, we were proud of his work and had seen his growth as a performer from the Spit Camp until the finals. Our 1st place winner was a grade 8 male who rapped about climate change. His look was priceless when he won; he was in disbelief that he beat out the Grade 11student. When it set in on him that he was the winner, his smile was stretched from ear to ear. In fact, all of the students were beaming with pride because they received positive feedback from the judges and a token of our appreciation. As educators, we need to remind ourselves that some of our youth don't receive positive reinforcement very often in their lives, for them to get a certificate or medal was a tangible accomplishment for them to show, and they held it with the same pride that an athlete does when winning their championship.

Our 1st place winner was not unique in that he was a junior, he was also a student at our First Nation alternative school. His teacher commented that she had worked with him for two years, but this working on his science-themed rap was the most excited and empowered she had ever seen him. She said that Science Genius would always be a good memory for him, mainly since high school can be a very challenging place for Indigenous youth.

The *Science Genius B.A.T.T.L.E.S.* program was a success in Toronto for many reasons including, supportive teachers, engaged students and because hip-hop is a culture that transcends all cultures. Students here in Toronto have a very similar connection to hip-hop as students from the Bronx, where hip-hop started. This program provided opportunities for our young people to engage in science differently.

CHAPTER 7

The Youth Perspective: My Experience as a Science Genius

Elicia Estime
@etheeemcee

My name is E, or you can call me E the Emcee, I am a Science Genius! My story begins during my freshman year of high school. I had just moved to New York from Miami and like many others was entering high school for the first time. Like every teen, I kind of had a cliché, melodramatic freshman year. I made a reputation for myself as a rapper from participating in cyphers during lunch to joining all the music programs my school had to offer. I wouldn't necessarily call myself popular, but I was known as "E," the rapper who came from Miami. I wouldn't say I'm the best rapper out there, but I am pretty good at my craft. So when the opportunity to create science-themed crossed my path, at the time I was surprised, like "wow people like my raps or bars?" as others might say.

It was one talk that lit the fuse for this whole Science Genius experience. It was around the end of the school year when 10th-grade science teacher, Mr. Lawrence, pulled me to the side to tell me about this "opportunity," an opportunity at the time I didn't know would change my life. Mr. Lawrence stopped me and was telling me how our school was selected to participate in a science rap competition, the *Science Genius B.A.T.T.L.E.S.*, and that I should join some of the 10th graders that year cause with all of our talents combined we could win the competition. He told me to come to his class during 3rd period on Friday and check it out and see if I would want to participate. Friday came along pretty quickly, and I made my way to Mr. Lawrence once the bell rang for the 3rd period. I sat down in a seat away from his class, and greeted the students that I knew and waited for him to tell me what to do. Once he instructed is class he came towards me and told me "she should be coming soon." My best friend Randy came and sat by me followed by my good friend Tre, and they asked me what I was doing in their class. I told them about the talk I had with Mr. Lawrence, and they told me how they were participating in the competition. A few moments later a woman walked in said hi to Randy and Tre as well as myself, but I could tell she knew them better. She chatted with them for a minute and then turned her focus on me. She introduced herself, her name was Brittany, and she was the ambassador of the *Science*

Genius B.A.T.T.L.E.S. for our school. I introduced myself and told her I would be participating the competition that year with Randy and Tre. After all the introductions we got started thinking about our science-themed rap. The guys told me that they wanted to choose atoms as the science topic to write the rap on. I know right, who raps about atoms? I was not feeling the topic at all, but I'm an optimistic person, so I was open to the idea.

1   The Writing Phase

Atoms. I was stuck here thinking about how I could write the hottest verse about atoms. I know, it's not that easy. I was having a severe case of writer's block, and first, it wasn't going too well. So, I decided I would write at home because I thought maybe I'll find a little inspiration there. When I got home I was still stuck, so I did what anyone would do if they were rapping about science, I did research. After reading numerous articles about atoms, I gathered everything you could know about atoms. Then I started writing. I would say my "aha" moment came right when I was about to give up. I was going to my writing process all-wrong, I was so focused on the information I forgot the most important part, my craft. So, I wrote how I usually do and incorporated the science little by little as I wrote. By the time I was done I had a complete science-themed rap that I was proud of.

Then, I got a call. I was in the middle of Regents' prep like I said before the year was coming to an end and many teachers were offering prep classes for the end of the year state test. I always took advantage of getting any extra academic support that my school offered. My phone started vibrating in my pocket, I pulled it out to see who was calling and it wasn't a number I didn't recognize. So, like any regular person would do when their phone is ringing, I stepped out and answered it. When I said hello a guy replied saying, "Hi, is this 'E'?" I said yeah, and then he told me who he was. He said his name was Edmund and that he was from the *Science Genius B.A.T.T.L.E.S.* program. He had got my number from Brittany and was verifying that I would be participating in the battles this year. Once I confirmed that I would be in the battles, he told me that I needed to be, at Columbia University and if I needed anything, anything at all gives him a call.

2   Rehearsals

Columbia University, "E" has arrived. Well "E" and Randy, Tre couldn't make it. Once we found where we were supposed to be we walked into a spacious room with tables and chairs and this massive projector in the front. There were a couple of contestants already there and as expect every school sat at a table by themselves. So, Randy and I sat at an empty table and just started chatting until this man walks in who dressed so sharp. I mean the guy had on a tux with not a crease in sight, clean tied shoes with the brightest smile ever. He greeted everyone, and it seemed like everyone knew who he was, even Randy. After saying hello to everyone, he took a seat right in front of Randy and I.me. He and Randy gave each other a dap. He introduced himself; he said his name is Chris and asked for my name. After the introductions, he asked us what we were working on, and if we needed help, we could always call him.

Then the infamous Edmund walked in. We all chatted and broke into sections to rehearse and perfect our craft. Honestly, the only issue we had was, picking a beat, so that's what we did. We spent rehearsal time finding an instrumental. As we're working a guy walks towards us, and he kind of looks like he's in high school. When he gets to us he introduces himself, he tells us his name is Jabari, and he was the previous the *Science Genius B.A.T.T.L.E.S.* winner. Randy told him that he remembered him from the competition and Jabari said the same. He was quite helpful in aiding us with finding a beat, but all the beats he suggested weren't working for us.

Then, I played an instrumental, Randy rapped his verse and I shared did mine, and it flowed. Then we had it; we finally found the perfect instrumental – Jay-Z and Kanye West's Otis instrumental.

3   **Competition Day**

You ever got on a rollercoaster, and right when you get to the top I mean the highest peak and the cart you're in slowly tips over into what you think is your death. Well, that's exactly how I felt that day, butterflies in my belly and my verse in my head on repeat. The competition was at the Intrepid Sea, Air, and Space Museum. Need I remind you I didn't know what the Intrepid Museum was or where it was but with the help of Google maps I found it. Come to my surprise it was a ship! The museum itself was a ship! When the guys and I got to the museum, and there were so many people waiting to get in and the lines were long. So, I wait in line with the guys, and I decided to call Edmund, we were performers and did not want to wait outside in line in the hot sun. So with one call to Edmund and a little direction, the guys and I got to pass all the long lines and security and was lead up by one of the museum employees. Need I say that it was awesome and I felt like I was famous, well I think that's how famous people felt at the time? We got to our designated location and saw Edmund and our competitors. We saw most of them at rehearsals, but there were a few unfamiliar faces. Moments later a guy who works at the Intrepid Museum walks in and hands us all get VIP passes. These VIP passes allowed us to have access to all parts of the ship without any problems. At that point, I was like this day can't get any better, but it most definitely did. I decided to walk around the Intrepid to see what the museum was all about and you won't believe who I saw, in the corner doing an interview – actor Derek Luke. No one knows how much I was overreacting in private. I ran to the bathroom and started acting like a crazed fan, I called my sisters up to tell them I saw Derek Luke. By the time I got out the bathroom and got myself together, it was time to rehearse. We all were told to wait backstage and rehearse one by one in private so that the other groups couldn't see our performance. So after what felt like years, it was our turn. Got on the stage and Edmund gave us each a mic, and when the beat came on, I was in my zone. Rehearsals went smooth, and the only thing that was on my mind was not to mess up during the real show. In the meantime, I would go back to exploring the Intrepid Museum. As I'm walking up the stairs to get out of the auditorium until Derek Luke stopped me. Don't worry I kept calm but on the inside, I was freaking out, he introduced himself which I thought was fun given I knew who he was already. He complimented me on my performance, which was huge especially coming from a celebrity, we chatted for a little shook and parted ways, which again I kept calm. After taking myself on a tour of the intrepid, all the contestants had to go on top of the ship to have a cypher.

Once we got backstage it was game time, Jabari walked in and told us how this would go. Our order would be based on the number we drew from a hat. Once the hat went around Tre pulled our number, and luckily we were close to last. Before the Final Battles began, I asked the guys to pray, because as a believer I believe all things are possible with God. So they were all for it, we bowed our heads, and closed our eyes and I lead the prayer. After our amen's the show began, and we just watched. Performance after performance, we watched our competitors then we were next.

It was our time to go up, as I walked up the steps entering the stage a mic was handed to me. I couldn't hear anything but my heart, at the rate, it was going I thought I would go into cardiac arrest, and then it went time. The Otis instrumental filled the room, and it was a switch, a switch that flipped on that made me feel powerful. I don't know if it was the music, or the mic, or the energy in the room but it was breathtaking and I let it take over. By the end of it, the beat was off, and I was left breathless, and tired and the crowd was wild. The cheers, claps and most of all my sisters scream I was satisfied and I didn't mess up. All that was left was the judge's decision. A couple contestants followed our performance, once they were through the judge's left to deliberate. The deliberation felt like years, and the suspense was killing me, and there they were. The judges were back, and this was it.

After long deliberation, it was a tie. A girl named Victoria who had done a spoken word piece about digestion won and everyone was waiting for whom the second winner was. I was holding Randy's hand, and my heart was beating outside of my chest. Honestly, I don't know what I was feeling. Then they said it, our school's name, *Brooklyn Community High School of Communication, Arts and Media*, that was us. We ran down shook all the judge's hands gave them hugs and stood there. I was shocked and I couldn't believe it, we had won. We were the 2014 the *Science Genius B.A.T.T.L.E.S.* winners. Oh, don't forget to cue the cameras!

4   Post Competition

Remember how I was saying this "opportunity," was an opportunity that at the time I didn't know would change my life, well here's how. Apparently, the guys and I were on magazines and blogs that we didn't even know about. Our picture and our story started emerging on all social media as well as the *Science Genius B.A.T.T.L.E.S.* program. After the competition, we were invited to be on Hot 97 radio show, be part of twitter conversations, and perform our track at many cool events. It was awesome! From kids to adults, everyone wanted to talk to us and take pictures. The experience was so surreal, it was a teaspoon of how being a celebrity would be like and I savored each moment. The experience was phenomenal, and I don't regret participating in the competition. I went from someone who didn't like science at all to now finding a way to incorporate it into one of the things I love, which is rapping. I enjoy science more after participating in the *Science Genius B.A.T.T.L.E.S.* program, and I now identify as a scientist, and I know I can do science. This experience is one I will never forget.

5   Today

I know what you're thinking, like what happened? Was that it? What are you doing now E? Well I'll tell you, as of today I'm a sophomore at my school, and if anything, Science Genius never stops. I am currently the ambassador for the *Science Genius B.A.T.T.L.E.S.* at my school, prepping some of my peers for the competition part of this life-changing experience just like Brittany did for Randy, Tre and myself. Chris and Edmund? Well, I talk to them almost all the time; especially whenever they're free, given they're busy people. Though when I do reach them, I'm always checking up on them to see if they're okay and vice versa. Would I do this again? Yes!! Without a doubt. I have learned so much from this whole experience and became a part of a family full of scholars, educators, mentors, rappers, producers and anyone who cares and wants to see young people make something of their lives regardless of their background. A family called #HipHopEd, which I can proudly say I am part of. Looking back if I did not participate in the *Science Genius B.A.T.T.L.E.S.* I would've never met Chris and Edmund. They are two people who I have not only grown so fondly of over the past year, but also care about dearly.

Both Chris and Edmund have been a few of the most genuine and caring people I have met in my life. Who always put others needs before their own. Every time I call them you know how they start and end their conversations with me? By saying, "if you need anything I got you." To some that might not seem like a big deal, but to me it means a lot. To me, it means that I have people who actually have my back and mean it too.

Chris, the creator of this project, has been a mentor and a friend to me. From rehearsals till now have always cared. Whether it was helping me fix my lyrics or advice on personal issues, I can always trust that my story is safe with him. That there are good intentions every time, he gives me advice, especially when I confide in him. Chris also supported my goals and dreams. As a rapper, not everyone helps you make your dreams come true, but Chris did. He hooked me up with shows and gigs around New York City, and I'm so thankful for them. Some say it's the effects of winning the *Science Genius B.A.T.T.L.E.S.*, and although that may be true, I believe it also had to do with him believing in my talent. He's someone who believes that everyone can achieve what he or she wants to, a great motivational speaker and a game changer. He inspires me to work hard and to be the best me that I can be. Chris is just an awesome person. Edmund, the coordinator of this project, has been a great friend to me. From the phone call that verified my spot in the battles till now, whenever I need him, he's a phone call away. So, because of that, one phone call to him helped me when I was sick, stressed, needed motivation and most of all an honest opinion. Edmund too has helped me in any way he can and aided me with opportunities that can lead to my success. He's an amazing and funny person too. Even if some of his jokes are a little harsh, there's never a dull moment; he's like family to me. Both of them are, but Edmund is someone who inspires me as well, how he works, goes to school, teaches, and does an abundant amount of things and he's still young. Inspiring.

I couldn't be happier with the decision I made to do the battles, and I don't regret it one bit. This experience was more than I can ask for and is one that I am still living until today. My name is "E," well I go by the name "E," and this was my *Science Genius B.A.T.T.L.E.S.* experience.

PART 3

The Intersection of Hip-hop Culture & Identity

∴

Tweets

∴

 Emily Bailin
@ emilybailin

The 5th element is esp. important for youth
during adolescence and identity formation
w/influences of media images & messages
#HipHopEd

 Hip Hop Psychologist
@drdla

The fifth element saved my life and gave
me a foundation to inspire others globally!
#HipHopEd

 Amil Cook
@amilcook

The Need 4 Us to Teach Ourselves our
Own History is Truly Essential &
Revolutionary! Knowledge of Self is Air for
Children #HipHopEd

 Brandon M. Frame
@brandonframe

Knowledge of self is important and essential
to growth and development. Through
carefully analysis of lyrics this can take
place. #HipHopEd

 DNLee
@DNLeeS

Giving kids permission to be themselves,
quirky, weird, & creative. Individual still but
part of a collective #HipHopEd

Introduction to Part 3: The Intersection of Hip-hop Culture & Identity

Christopher Emdin and Edmund Adjapong
@ChrisEmdin and @KingAdjapong

One of the fundamental arguments made by those who engage in and with hip-hop is that it must be recognized as a culture. At the same time, one of the chief critiques of hip-hop is that it sits on the periphery of existing culture and adopts norms/rules that seem to be contradictory to those that have been established by/in society and dominant culture and therefore cannot be seen as culture. This conundrum is one that cannot be easily settled. How can one group who sees something in one way convince others who are witnessing the same phenomena that it is something else? The answer lies in the recognition of not just the artifact being consumed, but the process that birthed its conception and its expression. How and why was it created? Who was it was made for? What is or isn't culture can only be determined by those who are experiencing it and can only be marginally understood by those who are witnessing it. When one witnesses another person's cultural expressions without participating in the culture itself, it becomes easy to invalidate its worth as culture. What is foreign about it becomes what is most prominent, and what is untraditional about it becomes what is most memorable. It is judged through the lens of the culture that one already has an allegiance to and its difference from that culture becomes used as a justification for why it is not a culture itself. This is what society has done to hip-hop, and why it is not always viewed as culture despite the fact that it has shown us consistently that it possesses all the attributes of any mainstream culture that the world validates. There is a reluctance in accepting hip-hop as culture, and even when it is accepted as such, a pejorative definition of culture is used. Rather than acknowledging hip-hop as a large force that encompasses the ways of knowing and being of a wide ranging yet intimately connected set of people with multiple identities, it becomes seen as a "residual category to explain unaccounted for variance in statistical model" (Lamont & Small, 2010). In many ways this contemporary view of hip-hop culture is a new iteration of the culture of poverty – which argues that social groups that have been marginalized from capitalist society will inevitable develop practices that help them deal with their oppression (Lewis, 1969). The issue with the use of this theory to make sense of hip-hop culture is that it positions hip-hop as always being about surviving and never about thriving.

Hip-hop then becomes bound by struggle for validation in the eyes of those who have the power to either validate or dismiss it as culture because of their preoccupation with their culture as a thing to be saved from being adulterated. Our view of culture in this part takes on a more Geertzian approach (not in a validating of Geertz as an absolute authority but rather as a provider of an interesting and useful lens to look at hip-hop). We see hip-hop identity and culture "... as suspended in webs of significance he himself has spun ... [and we] take culture to be those webs" (Geertz, 1973, p. 5). In other words, participants in hip-hop culture spin their ways into the culture and experience it in different ways not necessarily in response to, or in search of value in the eyes of some more powerful purveyor of culture outside of them, but because they choose to. They are bound to each other and become part of the culture based on their understanding of what hip-hop is and their relationship to it.

In an era where being a part of hip-hop culture has been demonized by society or relegated to being a fad for a segment of popular culture, those within the culture fight vigorously to retain our cultural identity. Unfortunately, what this has done is push many who have spun their webs towards deep engagement in hip-hop to be critiqued for their lack of appropriateness or decorum in worlds beyond hip-hop.

In this part, the chapters interrogate culture and identity with a consideration of the many unique identities that come together to create and enact hip-hop culture. Despite, and perhaps because of the uniqueness of the identities of the authors, they connect intimately to hip-hop. However, because of those same unique identities, they face circumstances where their hip-hop identities are not valued or respected. In the first chapter of this part, Matthew Morris, a educator in Toronto shares his experiences when he was a first and second year teacher who identified with hip-hop. Matthew describes the tension he felt around expressing his hiphopness. He expected that his school leadership and colleagues would not be accepting of his authentic hip-hop identity, and therefore he concealed it for years. He later realized how powerful a tool hip-hop can be when engaging young people, and began working though his understanding of how the field of education viewed him as a Black male educator who uses hip-hop anchored approaches to engage his students. In the second chapter, Kai Jones, an English educator in New York City schools shares how she grew up as a woman identifying as part of hip-hop culture. In her chapter, Kai discusses why and how she uses hip-hop text to engage her students in her English Language Arts class. In the third chapter of this part, Francesca D'Amico-Cuthbert discusses how hip-hop can be used to create a space within Toronto schools where students of color can feel a sense of belonging. Francesca also discusses the possibilities and limitations of using hip-hop culture to combat high dropout rates in Toronto public schools.

In the fourth chapter of this part, Jeremy Heyman explores his identity as an individual who follows Modern Orthodox Judaism and is a #HipHopEd(ucator). As a science educator who works primarily with newly arrived immigrants who are also English Language Learners, Jeremy shares how his realization of how influential hip-hop was among his students served as the catalyst for him to use hip-hop lyrics to encourage students to be critical of the inequalities that they face. Finally, in the last chapter of this part, Lauren Kelly reflects on the development of her hip-hop identity over the years. Lauren shares how her personal experiences around hip-hop have shaped her as an educator. In this part, the chapters interrogate the ways that culture and identity merge to bring educators to enact transformative practices in their classrooms while making hip-hop central in their pedagogy.

References

Geertz, C. (1973). Deep play: Notes on the Balinese cockfight. In C. Geertz (Ed.), *The interpretation of cultures: Selected essays* (pp. 412–453). New York, NY: Basic Books.

Lamont, M., & Mario, L. S. (2008). How culture matters: Enriching our understanding of poverty. In A. C. Lin & D. R. Harris (Eds.), *The colors of poverty: Why racial and ethnic disparities persist* (pp. 76–102). New York, NY: Russell Sage Foundation.

Lewis, O. (1969). The culture of poverty. In D. P. Moynihan (Ed.), *On understanding poverty: Perspectives from the social sciences* (pp. 187–200). New York, NY: Basic Books.

CHAPTER 8

The Art of Teaching Using Hip-hop

Matthew R. Morris
@Callmemrmorris

Because hip-hop is more than music, words, beats, and dance so to must be the ways in which we teach hip-hop. Hip-hop is a culture, manifest out of pain, othering, and expression. Like any other culture, grappling with it in order to reproduce and regenerate its forms can prove elusive. That is because, unlike any other culture, hip-hop culture has built-in detections to the unauthentic. This is also why merely photocopying lyrics to Tupac's *Keep Ya Head Up* in order to teach a group of students themes vital to any high school English class will lack any true connection if both teacher and students' entry points with the culture are not acknowledged. Before we mainstream strategies that infuse hip-hop into the curriculum, we must understand that the culture of hip-hop precedes any of its ligaments. When we keep this understanding in front of us, the art of teaching hip-hop becomes easier and more practical.

Christopher Emdin expounds upon the idea of teaching towards a hip-hop culture in the classroom in his *Ted Talk* titled "Teach teachers how to create magic" (2014). In his talk he alludes to "master teachers" who have the skills to teach and engage audiences but makes note that most of these people "may not have the degrees to be able to have anything to call an education" (Edmin, 2014). This piece would be shorter,or perhaps not even necessary, if we could change the processes of teacher certification and provide pathways for some of our more engaged and engaging adults to become public school educators. Since we can't change policy at this precise moment, let us continue to have a dialogue about what the art of teaching hip-hop is and how to better educate our educators on teaching through a hip-hop lens.

I must be honest with myself. I should use more hip-hop resources in my classroom. I have taught the 7th grade for the last two years, educating my homeroom class in math, language, and geography while also teaching science to the 7th grade cohort of my school during the afternoon. I have used hip-hop music to teach figurative language, thematic topics, and poetry in English class and have also implemented *Science Genius B.A.T.T.L.E.S.* at my school. I could use more tangible resources in my teaching practice. However, I don't feel obligated to for a simple reason. I have alternate ways of teaching hip-hop besides resources. Through the articulation of my intrinsic relationship with hip-hop I am able to teach much of the curriculum through my understanding of hip-hop culture and how it holds the potential to connect and inspire.

In my second year of teaching, as I finally became comfortable in my skin I couldn't deny any longer that I was part of a culture that had long been silenced in education. I had all the same degrees as the rest of my colleagues and could connect with them on all things pertaining to education (for the most part), but where I found a disconnect was through lived experience. As I learned how to become a teacher, I found myself emulating my peers and the veterans in the building; their style, their discipline, their demeanor. I had started emulate whether I agreed with it or not, simply because I thought that was *teaching*. There was also a time at the beginning of my career where, instead of listening to the music I liked coming into work, I would listen to talk radio. And I didn't listen to it because I had grown "older" and developed a liking for the latest news and sophisticated conversations. I was listening to talk radio on my way into work because I wanted to "learn" how to talk "white" or "professional" or whatever other term we use to describe racist rhetoric (partially learned through schooling, by the way).

Early in my career I *tried* to talk differently. In fact, I tried to talk like how a teacher *ought to talk*, informed by my prior experiences about the school system. As I got more comfortable in my role, I got more agitated with the veil I was purposely concealing over my true identity. I also realized that this sort of attitude was perhaps sending wrong messages to many of my students, especially the marginalized ones.

By neglecting my own culture in my own classroom, I was contributing to a historical source of internalizing conflicts that fostered so many Black students' disdain and disregard for school. I felt that I was creating a gap in the connection between the students who I taught and more importantly, those ones that looked up to me. So, I began to consciously sound like myself, and by extension, not really sound like any of the teachers around me. It was noticed, at first by one of my younger Black students, Shaun, who came up to me one day during science class and said, "you talk more like my uncle than my teacher." I swallowed his outward views without coming to a conclusion of whether it was a compliment or a criticism. Ironically, his comments initially stung me. I thought that perhaps I was becoming too "unprofessional." But instead of folding my hand I decided to push my chips all in. I was ready to experience what embodying the art of teaching through my prescribed hip-hop identity would truly become.

For young, Black, male teachers, the issue of developing an identity is one of tremendous importance. It is a luxury for others, namely white males and females, to not contemplate this phenomena as they enter the profession of teaching. Identity, as it stands, is one of the most, if not the most, crucial foundational aspect for any new teacher. For young Black males entering the teaching profession, it takes on additional importance. I took my first step in becoming a "Black" teacher by establishing my own voice with full understanding that sincerity demonstrates authenticity. Many fundamental "lessons" are taught to students, hidden way beyond the curriculum. I felt it my duty to bring more of these implicit schooling measures to the light. Far from my first day where I was reluctant to even put my earrings in that morning, I began to grow into the educator that I wanted to become.

The merger of the young, urban, Black Matthew R. Morris and the teacher Mr. Morris was a treacherous path. I earned more degrees in education, obtaining my Masters and school leadership certification. While I did that, I clung to my "seemingly" escaping identity by getting more tattoos. The idea of "being shaped" and, equally as detrimental, being jaded, by the profession frightened me to the extent that I were I once thought my little tattoo on my bicep would cause parents angst in a parent-teacher interview bulged into showing up for Meet-The-Teacher nights in a t-shirt, jeans and Jordans, with tattoos on both arms down to my wrists. Ultimately, I kept the students my first and foremost priority. Firmly grounded in my confidence to deliver a hip-hop pedagogy without necessarily relying on hip-hop texts, I had reached a point where anything short of striving for this action would not only devalue my worth as an educator but the worth of many of my students.

When I teach now, regardless of what it is, I teach through hip-hop. That is because hip-hop culture is the chief culture I grew up with. The art of teaching hip-hop, when one peels back its layers, can become simple: if we want our students to engage with school, then we must meet them at *our* entry point with *their* culture. Make no mistake, hip-hop culture is youth culture, regardless of how entrenched we are as adults, or "OGs," with it.

This is especially true for educators who work in inner cities. They will find that the majority of their students, regardless of race or socioeconomic status, cling to hip-hop culture. Whether it is through the music or articulating the culture through dress and dialogue, these students are walking embodiments of a culture that is historically excluded and ostensibly denied from traditional schooling. How ironic is it that the most influential culture amongst today's metropolises is explicitly uninvited into the classrooms and hallways of our most important institution – the school? It is our job to unapologetically request for these forms of culture not only to be invited in, but cherished and prioritized amongst the conversation that re-conceptualizes schooling methods. And we can do this not just through a suturing with hip-hop texts and curriculum, but with the actual methods of how we teach.

Teaching is about creating connections with students in order for them to learn material, tools, and ideas that will foster self-esteem, self-worth and

ultimately allow them to become successful into adulthood. But before they
begin to "work" for you, you have to bridge a gap between yourself and the
student in order for them to actually do the work necessary in the present
moment that will lead to an eventual prosperous relationship they will have
with education. That takes three aspects of a hip-hop pedagogy – developing
an identity in the classroom, building connections through communication,
and extending oneself as an educator.

Developing an identity in the classroom can be a volatile affair if spoken
about in vague terms. Merely encouraging educators to "be themselves" can be
double-edged if that advice is not followed with practical wisdom on how to
check our privilege and biases. We all come to educational spaces with biases.
How we negotiate those biases is critical if we want to connect with all of our
students in a way that validates their experience as individuals. We cannot
simply encourage educators to "be themselves" in the classroom if their views
about particular bodies and the way they negotiate personal relationships
based on those views inform their pedagogy from a perspective that negatively
taints student learning, validation, and outcomes. Instead we must facilitate
opportunities for *all* educators to challenge their preconceptions, teaching
practices, and methods of engagement. This is where hip-hop culture as a tool is
become especially useful. Developing an identity as an educator is not a process
that ought to happen in silos but instead should emerge through a collective
process that includes community members, individuals within academia, the
public school, and the policy makers, and of course, our students. Developing
one's identity as an educator must be truly collective and reflective if we want
to transform modern pedagogy to include hip-hop's most vital aspects.

Because hip-hop is the culture I clung to since childhood, my identity as
an individual eventually superimposed upon my identity as an educator.
That is a positive. I *chose* to wear *fly* sneakers, stressed jeans, and scoop tees
to work. This is one part of a hip-hop aesthetic that manifest itself within
my identity that makes "connecting" with my students *somewhat* easier. But,
I must emphasize that I *choose* to wear urban markers of aesthetic within a
conservative educational environment because it is merely how *I* like to dress.
What one wears can never indicate one's connection to hip-hop culture.
I would be the same reflection of hip-hop culture if I chose to wear plaid shirts,
dress pants, and bowties to teach every day. Point being, aesthetics can be a
marker but the art of teaching hip-hop is incredibly more complex than just
clothing or music preferences.

When I first started teaching I was afraid to wear my earrings into the
school. I was anxious about leaving my polo untucked or wearing a short-
sleeved shirt that would expose the tattoos I had on my upper arms. Perhaps
the unconscious micro-aggressions I had received as a high school student,

and then again in undergrad, prevailed over my notions of how to navigate my own representations. As I became more comfortable in my position I started to reflect my identity more authentically. And it is authenticity that is key when we chose to incorporate a hip-hop pedagogy within our classrooms. Teaching teachers how to teach with a lens that acknowledges their bias, emphasizes their identity, and opens entry points between their lived experiences and the experiences of their students is, in effect, hip-hop and everything that our culture is about.

When one is able to develop an authentic identity that acknowledges those three things mentioned in the previous paragraph it naturally extends to an enhanced ability to create connections through communication. In his book, *Beats, Rhymes and Classroom Life*, Marc Lamont Hill speaks about an experience he had as a graduate student researcher slash alternative-education high school teacher once, when he felt compelled by the direction of a particular classroom dialogue and decided to share *his own* story in an authentic and vulnerable tone. The encounter was a high tide moment in his classroom and one that forged relationships and a classroom dynamic that students would often recall in later class sessions. In recollection of this moment, he writes, "Although my power to end the conversation when I deemed it appropriate affirms that I never completely ceded my authority as teacher, there was nonetheless a moment in class when I felt as if my story was no more or less important than others" (Hill, 2009). When it comes to teachers sharing personal stories, or what I would more accurately describe as creating connections through communication, most teachers who work today could rarely speak about an experience in which they divulge personal information in front of a classroom full of their students. Yet, we hope to build authentic relationships amongst our students and expect them to blindly take any advice we give them. We want our students to relate to us but are unwilling to move off of our savior-like self-image and actually *share* our own stories with students. Rather, we assume we are fulfilling the deed of the quality educator by simply listening to our students' stories and advising them from some omniscient vantage point of the "objective" teacher. The student-teacher relationship is not in such a flailing state yet, but with increased standardized testing and progressive policies that push the teacher into more of a robot-like role, the future of the classroom doesn't look the most hospitable. Fortunately, the art of teaching hip-hop provides a mechanism for pedagogy that can be revolutionary to our archaic state of instructional practice.

Hip-hop is arguably the most expressive and self-reflective form of music. These artists gain influence through sharing their own personal stories and will also catch flack when accounts of "ghost-writing" of falsehoods in their persona are unearthed. If we want to connect with our students, especially our most marginalized, we must infuse these ideals into our pedagogy as teachers. Hip-hop culture, in its art for introspection, reflection, and personal communication becomes a pedagogical baseline for basic instruction. Sharing personal stories, teaching from a contextual lens and speaking from an authentic voice are three ways that lend themselves to doing just that.

Connecting with students through authentic forms of communication can also be practically prescribed to educators. We must be willing to draw from our students' experiences; we can do this by intersecting our pedagogy with their experience culturally, contextually, and through community. Whether that is through the forms of explaining curriculum objectives and teaching lessons by using urban colloquialisms, re-engaging the class with subtle but poignant catch phrases that draw upon their culture and the content of the curriculum, or using hip-hop texts and community references as a foundation for delivering curriculum, we must open multiple pathways for urban students to see themselves reflected in the education they are supposed to digest. In this sense, connecting with students through authentic communication, whether it is story telling or cultural and community references provides educators with an opportunity to validate the notion that one's personal knowledge should always contextualize, or make sense of, the curriculum. Hip-hop makes meaning out of the personal. The art of teaching hip-hop must use one's personal epistemologies to make meaning out of curriculum. This pedagogical framework validates learning and emphasizes the idea that we all come to knowledge through our own entry points. Through understanding and using the art of hip-hop's ability to communicate an authentic narrative of oneself and community, we avoid impeding academic achievement and instead foster it.

And by extension the first two aspects of improving one's pedagogy through the art of teaching hip-hop leaves us at extending oneself as an educator. Naturally, when we develop an authentic identity through acknowledging our own biases while converging with our students at our multiple entry points of hip-hop culture done through effective communication, we will extend ourselves and our practice for the better. Actually, we cannot perform the first two pedagogical initiatives without firstly performing the latter.

In order to teach through the art of hip-hop culture we must connect with "roots." That means going out and learning the community you work in, familiarizing yourself with the discourse and culture your students (re)produce, and humbly acknowledging your inadequacies as both a teacher and an "understander" of all your students' knowledge. You don't know have to memorize verses of the latest hip-hop tracks to gain familiarity with the culture or your students. Instead, simply asking your students what they listen to, taking some time out to have a conversation about their cultural interests such as their latest musical taste may suffice. I teach in the city of

Toronto, where since 2008 and hip-hop artist Drake's rise to fame, the city has seen tremendous growth as an autonomous cultural force on the hip-hop scene. With the likes of Drake, The Weeknd, Nav, and Tory Lanez to name a few, Toronto's hip-hop scene has bubbled to an unprecedented level. This is indeed reflected in the youth I teach. Thus, despite my Jordan's, or earrings, or tattoos, I still represent a hip-hop culture that is somewhat dated and stale. The students in my building fill their iPods with songs from artists I, in all my hip-hop "savvy," have never heard of. But that does not stop me from taking time out of my day, whether it is a break in between a lesson, sitting down with a group of students while helping with some math, or during lunch while I spend my supervision duty escorting students out to the recess fields asking questions about what's hot and who is dope right now. Hip-hop culture, like the cultural landscape of education is always evolving. As educators, we must be willing to simultaneously enter, understand, and interrogate both of these spaces if we truly want to build connections with students and foster academic achievement. The game of education and that of hip-hop should no longer be mutually exclusive if we are real about the achievement gap we vow to finally close.

"What I'm 'bout I represent it" (Hot 97, 2017) is a line that famed rapper and member of the Roots band, Black Thought, freestyles during a Hot97 radio program in late winter of 2017 hosted by Funkmaster Flex. The entire ten-minute freestyle is rich enough for an entire chapter but it is that line that resonates with the notion of the art of teaching hip-hop. Ultimately, we must be willing to represent our students through learning, emphasizing, and finally valuing their culture within our curriculum. We can do this through many methods; using hip-hop texts, fostering more contextual frameworks for learning and student engagement that center the hip-hop experience, and coming down of our conservative pedestals as "teachers" to connect as people. When we revise our paradigms for education to reflect more inclusive practices through strategies like differential assessments of learning, dissolving narrow school policies like dress codes, and re-creating teaching strategies and methods that put student's realities, cultures and experiences at the center, we will see an altered and more practically-improved landscape for public education. With these strategies, I have no doubt that we will see improvements to both the quantitative data on student academic success and the qualitative data on student school experience, especially as it relates to our black students.

As a teacher, approach to student learning has changed from my first year to my seventh. As a young Black male over seven years ago, I naively thought that my mere presence would serve as enough to connect with and inspire my black students to learn. For some it did,ut for others, I learned that I had more work to do. Simply being a Black male teacher doesn't mean you are going to get black male students to "learn." But Black male students not demonstrating learning doesn't mean that those same kids are not incredibly smart. We must fully take responsibility for the disparaging achievement gaps that exist for some racialized groups and come back to the drawing board with proposed changes, based on student voices and statistics, and devote ourselves to finally plugging the gap that leaves many black students feeling like school "is not for them." We have been on the same train for decades now, hoping that it will take *all* of us, even our most marginalized to the destination of academic and social well-roundedness. But that train has never really left the platform for many students. It is time to get on the new one.

References

Hill, M. L. (2009). *Beats, rhymes, and classroom life: Hip-hop pedagogy and the politics of identity*. New York, NY: Teachers College Press.

Hot 97. (2017, December 14). *Black thought freestyles on flex | #freestyle087*. Retrieved January 08, 2018, from https://www.youtube.com/watch?v=prmQgSpV3fA

Hip-hop Education: A Perspective of the Culture through the Eyes of a High School Teacher

Kai Jones

Growing up in Jamaica Queens, in a low-income neighborhood, hip-hop surrounded every aspect of my life. Every day was a constant reminder of the love that not only I, but the people around me had for it. It was present in the way we dressed, spoke and walked. The sounds of Public Enemy, N.W.A and of course Queens rap Legends like Run DMC and LL Cool J blasted through the courtyard during hot summer nights. I did not choose hip-hop, hip-hop chose me. It called me, and spoke directly to me. Hip-hop was relatable growing up in a neighborhood surrounded by drugs and violence. When I listened, my story was portrayed accurately through the words. It was and still is a part of my culture and identity. As I grew, although familiar with other genres of music; including the old school rhythm and blues and jazz my mother played on Sunday mornings or the reggae tunes heard on 98.7 Kiss FM Sunday nights, impeccably mixed by Bobby Konders and Jabba, there was no other genre I would have considered my own. Hip-hop was the genre of music that I felt represented me, my friends, my neighborhood, it was and is my everything. The lyrics taught me about life, and unlike the opinions of rap opponents, who often viewed rap as negative, I knew of no negativity that rap promoted because it was my reality.

1 My Love for the Genre

It was in 1988 when my sister introduced me to the Great Adventures of Slick Rick. I was mesmerized by the catchy lyrics. I devoured it, dubbing the tape on my cassette player because my sister didn't want me to ruin hers by continuously playing it. I listened, rewound and wrote down the lyrics until I had memorized the entire cassette. I can't say I understood all of its contents; nonetheless, I was intrigued. It was through Slick Rick that I realized that hip-hop was more than just music, it was art. In school many of my peers also listened to hip-hop, it was our connection. We were able to relate to each other through it. We discussed it on the bus and at the lunch table. When new songs

© KONINKLIJKE BRILL NV, LEIDEN, 2018 | DOI 10.1163/9789004371873_013

dropped, we would come in and compete with who knew the lines better. It was a bonding experience for us. It excited us.

However, in class, hip-hop was never represented. Even in music classes, hip-hop was painfully absent. Although it did not stop me from learning, it did teach me at an early age how necessary it was to code switch. I learned quickly that my dialect was not the one of the mainstream and therefore was not acceptable in specific settings, including the classroom. What was acceptable in my neighborhood was not acceptable in my gifted and talented class at school. The music I listened to was foreign to my teachers who were of different backgrounds than me. The language used in the songs I heard and the words and phrases I spoke when I was amongst friends, was referred to as "incorrect" English by my teachers. Unfortunately, during this time, hip-hop had not yet gained popularity or acceptance among the masses and schools did not represent my culture in daily lessons. Thinking back, the only time I learned anything about someone who looked like me in school was during Black history month where the usuals; Martin Luther King Jr., Harriet Tubman and Rosa Parks were on display, and book reports were assigned to ensure we understood the importance of Black history. And although they are prominent figures in African American history, and despite the fact that I was thankful that they at least looked like me and deeply did so much for the "Black struggle" they still were not a full representation of where I was from.

This is a common issue among youth who are from the hip-hop generation. Their heroes and idols are erased from both Black history and everyday life. It causes an alienation from school and a disconnection from schools and schooling. In many cases it causes them to question their identity and its value in schools. Both boys and girls learn to enact problematic views of gender that go untroubled by schools and have no space within schools to envision a view of self that has true worth. In my case, it wasn't until middle school that I formed a connection to females and their power and strength. Ironically, I found this through an appreciation for female hip-hop artists. Salt-n-Pepa showed me that ladies could also navigate the male-dominated field. From their lyrics, I learned about feminism and the right for women to be who they are with no remorse. Mc Lyte taught me it's okay to speak my mind and Queen Latifah taught me U.N.I.T.Y and not to accept any form of disrespect. They gave women a voice that I never knew existed. I thought if they could rap about these things then for sure it was ok to express my feelings. Not only did their lyrics influence my culture, but my fashion changed as a result of female rappers and the images they portrayed. I also mimicked their hairstyles, my feathered cut in my eighth-grade school photo could prove it! I can only imagine what it would've been like if these positive images were welcome in the schools I attended and allowed to be a part of the curriculum. These were females who were, as we would say then, Dope! Bringing them into the classroom would have allowed me to see school as dope as well.

My love for hip-hop didn't end with just listening and enjoying the lyrics. My friends and I formed our own girl's rap group. Even though we didn't make it very far, the inspiration that came from watching women take charge allowed us to try. We would gather at each other's houses, share our ideas and begin to write our lyrics. We would perform in front of family and friends. It was more than just rapping; it was also a form of bonding and our chance to tell our stories. Once our rap group failed, we decided to start a dance group that ended up being much more successful. Dancing to different mixes of hip-hop tunes, entering competitions and practicing day in and day out was a critical part of my childhood. It was a time that I learned some of the most valuable lessons of my life; teamwork, dedication, never quit and failure is not an option. Once again, hip-hop was/is not just about rap; it was culture. It's not negative; it's some people's reality. It doesn't cause violence; it brings people together. Literally, a DJ, (like a dancer or an MC), could save a life! It saved mine.

2   Why Do I Teach Hip-hop in My Class?

The most vivid memories I have from my many years of schooling in New York City public schools revolve around my recognition that the teachers I had were not a reflection of me. I could not relate to my teachers on a level any deeper than the fact that they were the teacher and I was the student. I never felt close to a teacher nor did I think that teachers, beyond elementary school, ever took the time to get to know me. I was self-motivated, and had parents who pushed education. Those two factors took me a long way. However, I had friends who did not have that support at home or school who ended up dropping out in either middle or high school. They didn't feel like they belonged in an educational institution because they weren't learning skills they could use in their real lives. In school, the absence of care and a value for their culture made them feel isolated and alienated.

It wasn't until my 12th grade year that I met an exception to what had become the norm. Her name was Mrs. Sirico; she was the only Black teacher that I recall having at this point in my education. Mrs. Sirico saw me. She recognized me not only as a student but a human being. She was the first person who took the time to compliment me on my writing skills and offer her assistance when it came down to choosing a college. She had attended NYU and offered to contact the dean if I was interested. Mrs. Sirico gave me confidence that I hadn't received before in school. What she offered was bigger than the gifted and talented programs I was in as a child. The expectation was always that I was to complete my work and do it well but teachers didn't take time to affirm me by showing me their human side; to relate to me. I always felt like this was essential but all became clear when decided that I would enter the education field late in my college career. As I decided on what I would do with a bachelor's in English, I recalled Mrs. Sirico, and I knew that teachers like her were not present enough in urban schools. I chose to return to New York City public schools as an English teacher so students could see someone that was a reflection of them. They would see someone who is hip-hop. When I began to teach, I realized that growing up in New York and attending public school gave me a relatability that was rare. I wanted my students to understand that they could be themselves and still be successful. They did not have to feel like they didn't belong or school wasn't for them. There are people, who are successful, who come from where they come from.

This thinking is what drove my desire to teach hip-hop in the classroom. Although the critics have often viewed the lyrics of hip-hop songs as being negative and are quick to point out the violence associated with hip-hop, these are the same people who do not take the time to study the history and social contexts of the lyrics and rappers (Blanchard, 1999). I, like my students, have a deeper connection to the art form. My students, in this day and age, have been exposed to much more than I ever was due to advancements in technology, and their constant use of social media. They understand that they are underrepresented in the education system, and can see and feel that they have teachers that neither look like them or value them. They understand that they are not represented in the curriculum. Hip-hop, despite the overwhelming effort to bring it into classrooms, is still not part of the curriculum in a number of urban schools despite research proving the benefits of incorporating students' cultural backgrounds into instruction. Overwhelmingly, schools have continued to stick to canonical texts such as *Animal Farm, Moby-Dick* and *The Catcher in the Rye.* As an English educator, to I do not discredit the value of these books but as a hip-hop educator, I acknowledge that they are missing cultural connections that are integral to connecting to children's lives and realities and should not be the only texts that children are exposed to. A few years back, in order to bring some diversity into the schools we were introduced to text such as; *In the Time of Butterflies* by Julia Alvarez, *The House on Mango Street* by Sandra Cisneros, *Monster* by Walter Dean Myers and *The First Part Last* by Angela Johnson. While these books these books presented the urban experience, they did so in a stereotypical way that still did not fully connect to the hip-hop experience. Some students devoured these novels, while others were not inclined to read the books because of what they considered a lack of authenticity or accuracy. These were the students that still were not being reached and always felt as if school was not representing them or their lives. Unlike when I was young, and pushed through with the support of my family, they remained resistant to learning the content with the use of the text being offered.

The use of new/diverse texts alone is not enough, and admittedly, simply merging hip-hop into the English curriculum isn't enough. After several attempts to draw content connections through the use of hip-hop; I realized that although my students enjoy the merging of the two, the concept that I was trying to teach through incorporating the use of hip-hop lyrics with canonical texts, was sometimes lost due to the students becoming more focused on the songs than the actual concept being taught. They instead wanted to discuss the lyrics and the meaning of them. They tried to relate the words and ideas to their own lives, telling their personal stories or make comparisons to other hip-hop songs and artist. Their responses brought back those childhood memories when my friends and I bonded through the lyrics of hip-hop artist. I realized "simply juxtaposing such texts with canonical texts in the classroom does little to rectify the cultural inequality that already exists in education" (Kelly, 2013). By only employing the use of hip-hop into a few lessons to try to reiterate points I was still feeding into the idea that hip-hop itself was not pertinent enough to teach in an English classroom setting. Using rap songs within a lesson was cool, but it still didn't validate the art form. It didn't validate my students. It didn't validate the culture. The act, although not intentional, communicated to them that their culture was not mainstream, that their culture wasn't allowed at the forefront of education. This was never my intent, so when I began teaching high school and given a chance to choose an elective, I decided to teach a hip-hop course, not the type of course that discussed the start of hip-hop or concentrated on a particular hip-hop era or artist, but this course focused on teaching English through the use of hip-hop lyrics. It would be a merge of English reading skills learned in contemporary English classes and instead of canonical text as the focal point, the lyrics of artists such as Jay Z, Kendrick Lamar, Kanye West and J. Cole served as the core text.

When I first developed my curriculum, I thought back to Slick Rick, the storyteller. I knew that hip-hop was more than just lyrics on top of a beat. Rap music has roots that originated in the African oral tradition and has for years given a voice to many of the voiceless and underrepresented groups in our society (Blanchard, 1999). Rap tells stories just like those in the required reading books.

3   Using Hip-hop in the Classroom

In the classroom, I try to offer what I never received while utilizing a structure for my instruction that aligns to what I have been trained to do as an English language educator. Instead of using literary text that disengages students,

I expand the notion of what text is, and anchor my instruction on using artifacts that have real meaning. When I use hip-hop, I pick songs that tell a story, and allow students to dig deeper into the content of the lyrics. As the students enter the classroom, the song for that unit is playing. I smile as they listen or sing along to the words when they are familiar with them. Some dance or bob their heads, others immediately begin to discuss. I ask the students if they are familiar with the song/artist, what they understand about the song by either listening or through their prior knowledge. I then pass out the lyrics to the song and play it again (or the video where available), this time allowing them to follow along as they listened. Students are then instructed to analyze the lyrics either with a partner or a group. They break the lyrics down verse by verse, notating in the margins as they would with any other text.

Next, we reconvene and discuss the annotations and decide on themes found within the lyrics; this becomes our catalyst for research and discussion that goes beyond what would have been generated with anything other than hip-hop

For example, on J Cole's song "Neighbors," Cole discusses the issue of racial profiling, even for someone like himself who reached a certain amount of fame. Lines such as, "Some things you can't escape: Death, taxes, and a racist society that make every ni**a feel like a candidate for a Trayvon kinda fate" (2016, track 7). These lyrics became a catalyst for discussions about racial profiling that otherwise would not have been brought to the fore. Racial profiling then became a prime focus of discussion and research; with students employing rigorous research techniques to interrogate and write about what they are researching. Specific cases of racial profiling such as the shooting of Trayvon Martin were discussed, and historical examples of men and women killed due to their race, including Black teens such as Emmett Till; and current events such as the racial profiling of Muslims in today's society became the focal point of classroom discussions. When engaging in these types of lessons, I ask students to locate supplemental articles based on the themes and contemporary issues discussed during the analyzing of the song. These pieces are used to support ideas and give factual information. I then supply additional materials that support the theme such as chapters from books that range from *The Autobiography of Malcolm X* to *Assata*. These texts are also explored in much of the same manner as the hip-hop verses are, and later used in addition to additional texts that help strengthen student arguments during a Socratic Seminar. At the end of the unit, students can choose to present the learned material in an innovative way which includes; rap, spoken word, poetry, drawing, sculpture, etc. The culminating event, after the unit is completed, is a celebration of their work and their talents. This process serves as an exemplar of the ways that hip-hop can be brought into the curriculum with a focus on culture while maintaining high academic standards and rigor.

4   The Critics

Critics of the genre that have direct impact on classrooms like school administrators and district personnel feel that there is no place for hip-hop in the classroom. Many of them view hip-hop as a negative influence in today's society. They think rap lyrics solely promote ideas of violence, misogyny, homophobia, the use of drugs and the glorifying of criminal behaviors. However, this thought frame and lack of understanding of other's culture is also what contributes to many teachers stereotyping Black students within their classrooms and labeling them as troublemakers (Emdin, 2016). It is essential to understand the culture of students in which we teach. Long gone are the days where the expectations were to do well in school and life, one must adopt the ideals of the mainstream culture. When you enter into someone else's space, you must respect all aspects of them and their culture and understand that different does not equate wrong. Historically we teach children that we are to fight for what we believe in and protect our civil liberties. We cannot then tell them that they can only fight when others deem it necessary. We cannot teach them their rights as American citizens in a history class, but contradict those rights within our own educational settings.

I am by no means saying that incorporating hip-hop into the curriculum will change society as a whole or change the views of all in regards to hip-hop and its culture. However, from the start of hip-hop in a Bronx neighborhood to now, hip-hop, no matter how negatively perceived, has become a global language. Through breakdancing, DJing and MCing and graffiti, the culture has brought youth, of all races, together. For me, and in my classroom, it has become the way to connect young people to nuance and beauty of English and literature. No longer is the art form associated with Black children in the ghetto. It has expanded to become the language and culture of the underrepresented. In a school setting, the underrepresented should be present within their education. By merging hip-hop into my English curriculum, I have only scratched the surface of what could be done within hip-hop education. Through the experience, I have gained a deeper understanding of the impact that a hip-hop curriculum could have on student ownership in learning as well as ownership in how they navigate through life in the future. It, in many ways, gave a voice to the voiceless. Through my curriculum, I was able to teach the students language, literary devices, history, societal issues and social activism. It broadened their understanding not only of English motifs but the world in which they live in, and how they can navigate through a society that has mislabeled, oppressed (whether consciously or unconsciously) and counted them out before they had a chance. To me, that is the true purpose of education.

References

Blanchard, B. (1999). The social significance of rap and hip-hop culture. *EDGE Ethics of Development in a Global Environment: Poverty and Prejudice: Media and Race*. Retrieved from www.stanford.edu/class/e297c/poverty_prejudice/mediarace/socialsignificance.htm

Chang, J., & Herc, K. D. J. (2008). *Can't stop won't stop: A history of the hip-hop generation*. New York, NY: St. Martin's Press.

Emdin, C. (2016). *For White folks who teach in the hood … and the rest of y'all too: Reality pedagogy and urban education*. Boston, MA: Beacon Press.

Hill, M. L. (2009). *Beats, rhymes, and classroom life: Hip-hop, pedagogy, and the politics of identity*. New York, NY: Teachers College.

Kelly, L. L. (2013). Hip-hop literature: The politics, poetics, and power of hip-hop in the English classroom. *English Journal, 102*(5), 51–56.

Seidel, S. S. (2011). *Hip-hop genius: Remixing high school education, leadership, and design*. Lanham, MD: Rowman & Littlefield Education.

CHAPTER 10

The "Northern Touch": Using Hip-hop Education to Interrupt Notions of Nationhood and Belonging

Francesca D'Amico-Cuthbert
@hiphopscholar82

On January 29 2008, Canada's largest school board in Toronto, Ontario voted to open an alternative school in order to pilot Afrocentric pedagogy, combat an estimated 40% drop out rate among Black teens, and establish a center for research on how to close the learning gap between Black students and their non-Black peers. Since 1995 when the province's Royal Commission on Learning suggested that a Black-focused school might help stem these statistics, and the city's school board reported that 40% of Caribbean-born and 32% of East-African born students in Toronto drop out of high school yearly, administrators have attempted to find strategies to address the issue. Today administrators, activists, and parents continue to argue that Canadian provincial curriculum is Eurocentric. This Eurocentricity leads school systems to overlook the heritage of Black students, with teaching failing to reflect racial diversity in their classrooms and to productively interact with Black students. During the 2008 proceedings, community leader Murphy Brown argued that due to the failure to incorporate even the most basic of African Canadian history instruction, Black youth are being pushed out of the system in what she calls a "school-to-jail-pipeline" (Brown & Popplewell, 2008).

Following the 2008 proceedings, Toronto education groups, both institutional and community-based, discovered that hip-hop curriculum retained the capacity to combat this exclusionary education model. Specifically, educators have recognized that hip-hop can alter educational outcomes by creating a transformative educational space where youth can become critically conscious of self as well as the effects of historical and contemporaneous structural inequities (Akom, 2009). This occurs when hip-hop exists as, what Education scholar D.T. Baszile calls a counter story. Baszile (2008) argues that in telling stories from the bottom up, hip-hop curricula attempts to uncover subjugated knowledge by speaking the marginalized into existence. Moreover, when students consume these counter stories, scholars, educators and curriculum designers agree that students are better able to analyze and challenge the logic of a Eurocentric model that works to maintain various forms of hegemony (Akom, 2009).

© KONINKLIJKE BRILL NV, LEIDEN, 2018 | DOI 10.1163/9789004371873_014

By using Canadian Rap music as a case study, this chapter suggests that one of the ways in which #HipHopEd challenges Eurocentric education and its outcomes is by engaging with the nation's master narrative of nationhood and belonging. In Canadian curricula, the master narrative is often reified through the stories the nation tells about itself through educational resources. Like Baszile, I argue that Canadian rappers, like their American counterparts, use hip-hop culture to create counter-stories that speak Canada's marginalized into existence and problematize the meaning of belonging and nationhood from their diverse perspectives. Once employed in the classroom, Canadian Rap possesses counter-hegemonic curricula potential in two ways. First, it offers students a transformative pedagogic space where they can uncover subjugated knowledge that challenges the logic of Canada's master narrative as well as the Eurocentric model of education. Second, it allows students the ability to consume contradictory responses to Canadian cultural hegemony that can aid in disarticulating the historical and contemporaneous contradictions of Canadian belonging and nationhood, as well as their place within this web of complex relations.

The potential of Canadian Rap to be incorporated into #HipHopEd constitutes what I have termed the "Northern Touch." In the 1998 recording titled "Northern Touch,"[1] Canadian rap group Rascalz asked listeners to, "check the lingo spread through the atmosphere [that is] so distinctive no other style comes near" (Rascalz, 1998, Cash Crop). The Rascalz (a multi-racial group) suggested that the "Northern Touch" was a unique style of performance, lyricism and musicality that differentiated Canadian Rap from its American counterpart. I will use "Northern Touch" as metaphor to suggest that Canadian rappers have a distinctive way of using rap music to speak the marginalized into existence to disrupt and disarticulate notions of belonging given the socio-historical relations particular to Canada. I will do so by first outlining the master narrative that frames the daily realities of Canadian citizenship, followed by a discussion of the ways in which Canadian rappers confront, through counter-stories, Canada's national discourse of belonging. In doing so, I suggest that Canadian Rap, when employed as curricula, contains within it transformative possibilities intended to encourage student engagement, and interrogate Eurocentric curricula and diversity both within and outside of the classroom.

1   Canada's Master Narrative: The State-Sanctioned Project
       of Multiculturalism

Canada's multicultural policy, first recognized by the Canadian Charter of Rights and Freedoms in 1982, is a state-sanctioned project that frames the nation as inclusive and its social relations as amicable. The master narrative of Canadian history has long dictated that the nation was founded by the competing interests of the British and French, that relations with the nation's Indigenous have been equitable, and that Canada continues to be a place of refuge for people of African descent. Historically Canada focused on being a nation where problems of racism, discrimination, and white privilege do not frame day-to-day social relations. Multiculturalism builds upon this national mythology in order to suggest that unlike the United States, Canada is a mosaic where its various racialized and ethnic groups comfortably co-exist, act collectively, and do not experience the pressure of assimilation. Political Scientist Jakeet Singh argues that multiculturalism is not simply a government policy but it has come to signify a normative vision for Canadian society. Singh contends that multiculturalism is construed as an extension of a "difference-blind" liberal approach to political inclusion and belonging where the chief concern is to create a neutral and impartial public sphere that deals equally and fairly with all citizens by favouring no particular identity (Singh, 2004).

Critics of multiculturalism, however, contend that the policy problematically frames into law who and how one officially belongs to the nation by concealing the nation's true social relations. Scholars argue that the policy creates inside/outside binaries by textually etching in those who are not French or English as Canadians, while simultaneously carving them back out through the construction of these individuals as static in their cultural practices and tangential to the nation (Walcott, 2003). Moreover, the federal policy has long functioned to conceal the social relations of domination at play and create a fiction that the modern nation-state is constituted from a "natural" sameness (Bannerji, 2000). While it is true that all groups have found themselves placed differently in the narrative of the nation this process has been constituted in the process of forgetfulness, coercion and various forms of privilege and subordination (Walcott, 2003). According to sociologist Himani Bannerji (2000), Canadian multiculturalism has always been a site for struggle and contestation in which the state's formation depends upon the conquering imagination of white supremacy, and a legacy of survival anxieties and aggressions in the form of colonialism, conquest, and exclusionary tactics.

In the context of African Canadians, multiculturalism has and continues to be problematically built upon a historical legacy of treating the Black Canadian presence with ambivalence. Historians like Robin Winks, Afua Cooper and Barrington Walker confirm that efforts to affirm African Canadian belonging have long ranged from reluctant recognition to their complete erasure from the national memory. Often framed as either 'newcomers' or a 'social problem,' Black Canadians continue to be imagined as adjunct to the nation (Walcott, 2003). According to Walcott, multiculturalism maintains the practice of concealing and denying otherness within the nation, while rendering acceptable the continued disenfranchisement of racialized Canadians. So much so says Bannerji (2000) that racism has become so naturalized and pervasive that it has become invisible to those who are not adversely impacted by state-sanctioned practices and institutions. Case in point, an education system in which racialized children continue to experience a sense of exclusion and its associated outcomes, while administrators, parents and community workers labor to name and confront this very system.

The section that follows builds upon the notion advanced by critics of multiculturalism that in order to combat racism and exclusion, it is necessary to re-imagine Canada through the presence of "others" who create counter-hegemonic discourses to expose Canada's real histories, social relations and the racialized code that produces Canada as a "white nation" (Walcott, 2003). Below, I think through how rappers have served as these "others," and I provide a series of examples in order to suggest the ways in which we might consider employing Canadian hip-hop as an educational resource intended to create counter-narrative moments in the classroom.

2   Canadian Counter-Stories: How Rap Music Interrogates Nationhood and Belonging

Many Canadian hip-hop practitioners argue that they first became attracted to hip-hop for its ability to re-imagine history and positively articulate Blackness. Rapper Maestro (formerly Maestro Fresh Wes) argued that among his greatest influences were Public Enemy and KRS-One who inspired him to, "be a man, [both] on and off the mic." These artists encouraged his knowledge of self. Maestro claimed that the work of rappers had educational value because it reinforced the need to learn about himself as a Black youth, the African diaspora and fostering an affirmative sense of Blackness.

In a 2012 interview, Maestro echoed a concern articulated at the 2008 Afrocentric school proceedings concerning the lack of racial diversity in Canadian classrooms and the absence of African Canadian heritage in the curricula. Maestro recalled his recent attendance at the Ontario Black History Society's Black History Month celebration, in which Zanana Akande, Canada's first black female cabinet minister, spoke about Canada's role in the transatlantic slave trade. Akande argued that Canada continued to perpetuate the myth that its involvement was as a 'safe haven.' She provided a counter-story that evening by contending that, "slavery widely existed in [...] Canada," and that "slaves – who in the minds of some still owe a debt – have been wrongly presented in literature as only the reapers of the generosity of a benevolent country" (Fanfair, 2012). She argued that this form of myth-making was, "due to a determined and an effective effort to control the story and hide the truth," and as a consequence she intended to, "retell the story [...] without the lines of omission." In recalling the event, Maestro claimed that it was not until the late 1980s, in his late teens and early twenties, that he was exposed to African Canadian history. This exposure, he claimed, did not come by way of his public schooling. Rather, outside of hip-hop and his home, there were virtually zero spaces that allowed him to re-imagine Canadianess in parallel to positively articulating Blackness.

In response to this gap, many Canadian rappers used rap as confrontational politics intent on redefining Canada's master narrative by situating Blackness as inherently belonging to the nation. Take the example of Choclair's 1999 debut album cover art in which he is pictured dressed in white, notably without a winter jacket, lounging in an ice armchair (Walcott, 2003). While the album title, "Ice Cold," employed the verbal strategy of signifying to reference his superior skills as a rapper, paired with the visuals, the term was also intended to provide a denotative reference to Canadian weather in service of re-imagining the nation (Walcott, 2003). Kardinal Offishall did this as well on his 2001 single "BaKardi Slang," when he claimed, "my style's off the thermostat, plus I'm coming from the cold" (Harrow, 2001). In each case, rather than simply reiterating the dominant national narratives of Canada as the 'Great White North,' a myth that is both a literal reference to winter and figurative reference to the nation as racially white, Choclair and Kardinal re-casted the tropes of White Canada in order to articulate a sense of self that mandates a rethinking of national boundaries and citizenship. In doing so, both artists located themselves squarely within the physical space of Canada, negating the claim that Black bodies could not withstand the harsh Canadian climate; a discourse that had long been used by immigration officials and policymakers as a reason to deny African Canadians access into the Canadian geographic space.

Canadian rappers have also re-imagined their "otherness" by employing the language of multiculturalism in service of valuing and unapologetically incorporating difference. In her first major release, rapper Michie Mee declaratively stated, "I am a Jamaican" in her 1990 single "Jamaican Funk (Canadian Style)." Part boasting record, the single was a sonic compilation of Rap and Dancehall that included moments where the rapper used Jamaican creole to lyrically interrupt and destabilize what the conflation of "Jamaican" and "Canadian" identities might mean, sound and look like. Through her lyrics, Michie positively affirmed her Jamaican-ness as central to her notion of self as both a Canadian citizen and a woman (Mee, 1991). The recordings' music video also promoted a series of positive articulations of Blackness. Interspersed with elements of street fashion and art, the Jamaican Funk video set was decorated with the thematic colors of red, black, green and yellow (references to pan-Africanism), Jamaican flags, and graffiti representations of ancient Egyptian icons, all of which were gendered as female (Mee, 2010). Canadian Rap has employed similar destabilizing strategies sonically by stating the influence and incorporating Canadian Rock through the practice of sampling. Though Canadian Rock has largely been understood as a white male genre (in relation to audience and practitioners), Canadian hip-hop practitioners have referenced the influence of Rock through the practice of sampling in order to insist upon their Canadianness. In Maestro's work for example, this music has included the work of Billy Squier, The Guess Who and Blue Rodeo. Maestro claimed, "[when] you asked me what type of music influenced me...I told you Rock, now that might have shocked you. We [hip-hop practitioners] love Rock. We're just being honest. I'm from Canada; beer, hockey and rock. That's how we grew up." Though Maestro cited the diasporic forms of Reggae, Calypso and Jazz as central to his musical upbringing in the home, he claimed that it was through schooling that he was exposed to Rock music. By referencing Canadian Rock as central to his musical vocabulary, Maestro, like Choclair, Kardinal and Michie, has used Black Canadian popular culture to destabilize a white Canadian trope, this time that of "beer, hockey and rock," by suggesting that this trinity is central to black Canadians as well.

One of the most valuable ways in which rappers have created counter-stories has been by explicitly speaking back to the hypocrisy of multiculturalism through lyricism. In one of Canada's greatest anti-racist Rap recordings "Nothing At All," Maestro argued, "we live in this place with racism called C-A-N-A-D-A. I'm watching it decay everyday. We got to hurdle the system, cause hate penetrates multiculturalism." Referencing the 1990 Oka Crisis, a land dispute between the town of Oka, Quebec and the Mohawk community of Kanesatake, Maestro claimed that Canada's language of tolerance was hypocritical and reflected an unequal treatment of racialized people. Linking the experiences of Canada's Indigenous people to African descended people, he contended, "the native man of the land is who you killing, and then you got the nerve to celebrate Thanksgiving. Framing every man as equal, I hate to see what you have planned for my people" Maestro Fresh Wes (1991).

When combined with the recording music video visuals, "Nothing at All" enforced hip-hop's instructive value. As the music video opened, viewers were treated to two competing scenes in which Maestro was featured encircled by broken hanging chains, and then encircled by a group of attentive multiracial youth while framed as an instructor. As the video cut between both scenes, Maestro's lyricism referenced a deliberate agenda throughout society to "mentally crush" the minds of the youth and "smother the dream of a black mind revolutionary regime." He claimed that these attempts ranged from the internalization of mental slavery, to the psychological violence of Canadian psychologist John Phillippe Rushton's racist scientific research,[2] and finally to the racial violence doled out by Canadian branches of the Ku Klux Klan. Stressing the necessity of knowledge of self among Canada's racialized youth, Maestro argued that young people should, "never let society distort [their] mind[s] away from comprehension," and that it was the duty of rappers to "reach and teach" the youth of these counter-hegemonic realities in order to empower them in the face of these master narratives.

3   Conclusion: Canada, Rap Music and Hip-hop Education Possibilities

At a time in Toronto education when racialized youth are dropping out at alarmingly high rates, hip-hop education proposes possible solutions. On the one hand, while hip-hop is a youth culture, it does not automatically speak to, or equally speak to all youth. As such, educators must recognize that hip-hop as pedagogy has limitations; by arguing that hip-hop is the best way to engage young people labelled 'urban youth,' we may be both relying on while making a set of assumptions that are unfair and even inaccurate, and as such possibly further marginalizing these students. This becomes a risky process, even as it attempts to act in a transformative capacity, particularly when educators fail to interrogate their classroom positionality and privilege, and most importantly the assumptions made as they design curriculum and pedagogy.

That said, hip-hop, when employed in a transformative way, and taken up by all students, even if unevenly, has the potential to help educators encourage critical thinking through a discussion of master narratives and counter-stories. As demonstrated through the example of Canadian Rap, hip-hop education has the capacity to aid youth in critically interrogating their world and place within it, particularly in cases where state-level messaging insists that Canada is a place they do not belong. By destabilizing notions of nationhood, educators can provide youth, particularly those who feel disengaged from mainstream Eurocentric education, with the tools necessary to interrogate a knowledge production process that continues to be, for many, inaccessible and alienating. Moreover, hip-hop.

Education can act as an outlet to express student curiosity and frustration and foster new meanings of place and belonging. Consequently, if education truly is an exercise in fostering the growth of a critically conscious citizenry, this is one of the many ways in which #HipHopEd can contribute to that project of liberatory praxis.

Notes

1 "Northern Touch," a single by artist Rascalz, featured fellow Canadian rappers Checkmate, Kardinal Offishall and Choclair. The single is considered a Canadian Rap classic and anthem that articulated the resilience and determination of the genre in a Canadian music industry that has long had a tenuous relationship with black music and musicians. The single became the first Canadian Rap song since the Dream Warrior's 1991 single "My Definition of a Boombastic Jazz Style" to garner widespread radio airplay both nationally and internationally, consequently reigniting interest in Canadian Rap music as a viable commercial endeavor.

2 In the 1980s and 1990s, Rushton, a proponent of the notion that racial differences in IQ are partially related to genetic inheritance, produced controversial research on r/K selection theory in relation to race and intelligence, race and crime and racial variation.

References

Akom, A. A. (2009). Critical hip hop pedagogy as a form of liberatory praxis. *Equity & Excellence in Education, 42*(1), 52–66.

Bannerji, H. (2000). *The dark side of the nation: Essays on multiculturalism, nationalism and gender*. Toronto: Canadian Scholars' Press.

Baszile, D. T. (2008). The oppressor within: A counterstory of race, repression, and teacher reflection. *The Urban Review, 40*(4), 371–385.

Brown, L., & Popplewell, B. (2008, January 30). Board okays Black-focused school. *Toronto Star*. Retrieved November 23, 2011, from http://www.thestar.com/life/parent/2008/01/30/boardokaysblackfocusedschool.html

Fanfair, R. (2012, February 2). *Blacks paid their dues in service to Canada*. Retrieved January 1, 2017, from http://sharenewsarchive.com/blacks-paid-their-dues-in-service-to-canada-%E2%80%93-akande/

Harrow, J. D. (2001). BaKari slang. On *Firestarter, Vol. 1* [CD]. Canada: MCA Records

Maestro Fresh Wes. (1991). Nothing at all. On *The Black Tie Affair* [CD]. Canada: LMR Records

Mee, M. (1991). Jamaican Funk-Canadian style. On *Jamaican Funk-Canadian Style* [CD]. Canada: First Priority.

Mee, M. (2010, August 7). *Jamaican Funk-Canadian style*. Retrieved from https://www.youtube.com/watch?v=ObqLwv7UtP8

Rascalz. (1998). Northern touch. On *Cash Crop* [CD]. Canada: BMG.

Singh, J. (2004). Re-articulating multiculturalism: Transcending the difference-blind liberal approach. In C. A. Nelson & C. A. Nelson (Eds.), *Racism, eh? A critical interdisciplinary anthology of race and racism in Canada* (pp. 444–455). Concord: Captus Press.

Walcott, R. (2003). *Black like who? Writing Black Canada*. Toronto: Insomniac Press.

CHAPTER 11

Rust Belt to Hip-hop: Development of an Emancipatory Science Knowledge of Self

Jeremy Heyman
@JHi86

When one envisions a hip-hop educator, my outward identity is probably not what pops into one's head; however, without each component of my identity combined with some happenstance coincidences of my post-high school life, I would not be here today writing this essay. Then again, my identity is at times full of unlikely combinations. If I had not chosen to follow Modern Orthodox Judaism, I would never have moved to Washington Heights or worked in the Bronx, where I have formed my adult identity. I have a passion for mentoring immigrant young adults in the likes of the Bronx, and while my grandfather came to Blairsville, Pennsylvania from Latvia as a boy, my home region has not exactly bubbled over with immigrants since the steel mills closed a few decades ago. I come from the Rust Belt of Western Pennsylvania, where most of my family has resided for over a century, where my father's family has long sold manhole covers and my mother's father worked as a dry-goods peddler and steel mill worker. The street where my family has lived for 35 years is flanked by forests on both sides, and my hometown of 29,000 is a place where people of different races and ethnicities, and of working and middle classes, tend to live and work in relative harmony to an extent not commonly observed in Pittsburgh or, as I would come to find, many other places.

This is not exactly a breeding ground for the hustle and bustle of hip-hop culture. Where I come from, New York City is a big city we saw on maps and on the news, and its culture of materialism, conspicuous consumption, and high cost of living were a seven-hour drive and mountain range away. My father came from a small, racially homogeneous, middle-income industrial town in the Allegheny Mountains. Prior to moving to a working and lower-middle-class Jewish neighborhood, my mother spent her early formative years in a neighborhood and elementary school where others, like her, came from families that were struggling financially, and where she was among the only non-African American students. She is the striver and matriarch of the family, marginalized at various points throughout her childhood and adolescence, but she focused on channeling the energy for good. My mom made sure we were grateful for everything that we had in our household, town, and school; due to a family member's illness, she had largely taken over running a household from age 14, working her way to a labor union scholarship to help her become a teacher. An elementary educator who used to teach reading at urban catholic schools out of a van until there was a shooting at one of the schools, for the past 20 years she has been teaching kids in our home district who cannot be in school for illness, injury, pregnancy, or criminal justice reasons.

From a young age, I enjoyed math and playing with pocket calculators from the likes of Big Lots. In high school, I was obsessed with all things science and mathematics. Science and math were my outlets for fun and expression, in the classroom and in activities from Math League to Science Olympiad, from the American Mathematics Competition to the Chemistry Olympics and Chemistry Olympiad. I never went out to parties or most other social gatherings, which was supported by being the only Orthodox, Sabbath-observant Jew in a high school of 1500 and a town of 29,000. Name recognition and branding are important in hip-hop, but I am pretty sure you have never heard of my hometown, unless you follow high school football or old 1990s Science Bowl rankings, prior to Westinghouse Electric's termination or relocation of most of its employees to more affluent suburbs. Still, we learned by middle school that we were to be grateful for the schools that we attended, as we were told that many other public schools were not as good as ours. Hip-hop capitalizes on profound written and oral expression, but English was by far the weakest department in our school, with perhaps our strongest English student falling asleep during the AP exam.

The script for academic success was relatively straightforward, and unless you played football, it was clear that academics were the key to moving forward. The top students were mostly South Asian students, a conglomeration of Sikh, Hindu, Jain, and Muslim kids from India, Bangladesh, and Pakistan, with a few East Asian and White students mixed in, and occasionally a Black student. Most of their fathers worked for Westinghouse Electric, and they wanted to become doctors or scientists. School was the first priority, we studied for many hours, and we did not allow ourselves to get caught up in drinking or smoking. Some kids did these things, some had their own kids, and the popular crowd was not exactly into studying, but the 4% of us who took all the advanced classes together steered clear of any of this. Maybe a couple of them did not, but if so, I was totally oblivious because I had goals, I enjoyed reading science books and doing problem sets, and I knew I had to work hard to earn college credits in high school and to get a good scholarship at a good college, the kind that people at my high school rarely attended, or even heard of.

I mention all of this background information because my reconstruction of it helps in understanding my evolution in college. I decided on Brandeis

University because it had very strong science programs, I wanted to be a member of an observant Jewish community for the first time, and I was blessed to receive a generous scholarship. One of my scholarships from a chemical society in Pittsburgh required me to be a chemistry major, and with the year of college credits I had earned in high school, I immediately declared my major and semester-by-semester plan to complete a 4-year Bachelor's-Master's program. I felt well-prepared because I felt that my high school was a very good one, and I had enjoyed being the top student or one of the top students in every subject in my high school, except English, the class that pretty much no one cared about anyway. When several of my friends got rejected from all the Ivy League colleges where they had applied, and they all decided to enroll at good public universities or second-tier local private colleges, I did not think much of it.

Overtime in college, I started piecing together the extremely different opportunities afforded to various friends and classmates of mine, seemingly based on their high schools, hometowns, and their parents' jobs. I had found out that of my 5-member high school Science Bowl team, representing the cream of the crop of science talent and motivation from my high school, the teammate who was first-generation to college decided to leave his four-year college after a year. There were a number of intelligent people at my high school, and dedicated teachers, but I remember when my calculus teacher spoke with a group of us at the end of 11th grade, as we had exhausted the school's math offerings a year early, and told us that she knew none of us would come back to live in this district, but that it was important to her that a good high school was maintained for "the others," for the majority who would not move on or out. I realized that my roommates and other friends in college almost always had at least one parent with a doctoral degree, and that many of them had gone to religious preparatory schools or very academically-oriented public schools. Some of them were not interested in studying science, which surprised me for a while on the basis of nearly all of the strong students I had come across in my high school. Far worse, some of my hall mates were smoking and drinking regularly, an activity that to me seemed irreconcilable with caring about school and being a responsible student and young adult. I learned that in one of the wealthy small towns near campus, drugs were actually popular, and I reasoned that the young people there had such a large margin for error that they could dabble in such activities while still being quite successful academically and having multiple doors open for a bright future. This idea of young people's margin for error ultimately became instrumental to my passion as an urban educator, but it is rooted in what I saw in the freshman dorms at Brandeis.

I also started learning about something that I would later find was called cultural capital. A lot of my classmates had an appreciation and understanding of classical literature, theater, and traveling to Europe for vacations, a collection at which I would shake my head and write off as the kind of "high culture" that my friends and I back home did not value. While science answered our questions about the world and was the key to solving local and global problems alike, this high culture just appeared to me as a useless separator of people on the basis of class rites and rituals. I had a professor ask me what he may heard of from my hometown, and when I mentioned football players, his response was, "No, I mean important things."

Part of this cultural capital was about connections to elite places and things, and part of it was also tied to the types of conversations that people had with each other. My mom and dad are college-educated and earned Master's degrees at night from a local state college, and growing up I knew I was grateful to be in a household where education was important, where homework was first priority, and where eating dinner as a family was important, even if it meant waiting until my dad made the 42-mile drive home from the foundry, and he was not home for so long before going out again to transport a couple manhole covers. On the other hand, dinner conversations were about things that to me seemed "normal," like all things Pittsburgh sports, the cake or cookies my mom would bake the next day, what competitions or tests I had coming up in school, how the garden was looking, and how the weather was looking. We did not delve into politics or literature, and the only things we debated were Pittsburgh Pirates roster moves, why the Pitt Panthers could not win in March Madness, or why my mom felt compelled to deliver a fresh cake any time one of us had a doctor's appointment. Much to my new friends' surprise, I did not go away to camp in the summer, and I had never used a passport. I had found religious commonalities with my new religious community in college, and I found friends with mutual interests in science, and I noticed that I had an easier time relating to the masses at Brandeis than some of my friends from urban schools.

As I became more conscious of class divisions in college, and became so fascinated with them that I was spending time analyzing my friends' home zip codes and high schools when I should have been sleeping or working on problem sets. I saw a lot of students getting weeded out of science majors and career aspirations, professors who lacked the interest or passion of my high school teachers while assigning work that was (perhaps consequently) several times more challenging and at times duller, and I started thinking about my own trajectory alongside that of my friends and peers. I met Professor Marya Levenson and took an Education & Social Policy class with her. The class spoke to all the issues and problems I thought of, and more that I had not thought of, and provided a bona fide academic space to discuss and work through challenges with an education system that I saw had so many problems with the role of "great equalizer" that so many of us naively thought had become true by the 21st century. Then I took a secondary education class with the same professor, and she placed me for my field observations in an urban science classroom, an experience that further shaped my interests and awareness of inequitable opportunities, as well as a growing awareness that I basked in interacting with individuals from diverse religious, racial, ethnic, and socioeconomic backgrounds. It was around this time that I also started listening to hip-hop and took an advanced inorganic chemistry elective with a young white professor from a poor urban neighborhood in Michigan, and I really took to his teaching methods as well as his occasional hip-hop references.

I became more and more incensed at the elitist and exclusionary nature surrounding the culture of my favorite disciplines in the ivory tower. My favorite toy as a child was a calculator from Big Lots, and in high school I enjoyed spending free time reading chemistry and physics textbooks and preparing for my Science Olympiad events, but I had known science as an enterprise that brought people together around solving problems for the common good, as in developing novel medications or pushing the frontier of our understanding of medical or environmental issues. If anything, it was subjects like English literature that seemed to be concerned with elitist ends, and consequently undeserving of my energy. Seeing intelligent and hardworking people leave science majors and career aspirations in droves, at least in part in response to various science professors with no investment in engaging, high-quality teaching and a lack of ability to connect with their students, was abhorrent to me. I was able to "make it" and I recognized that my high school chemistry teacher had conditioned me to the level of hard work necessary for success (and I had the good fortune of attending a high school where that was possible), especially as complemented by the emphasis that my mom placed on schoolwork always being my predominant priority as a teenager; however, I felt an impending sense of empathy for the "other," for students who were marginalized in the sciences and often came from neighborhoods and schools at the other end of the spectrum from the prep-school kids.

My growing frustration and desire to fight back against the unwelcoming culture of science in the ivory tower helped me in my decision to leave the laboratory lifestyle in favor of teaching ESL-infused chemistry classes at ELLIS, a new public high school for over-aged recent immigrant students who were new to the English language in the Bronx, NY. I moved to a predominantly Dominican neighborhood where many of my students also lived, and without having a lot of friends around me in the never-greet-others materialistic metropolis of New York, my students ultimately became an integral part of my new community and life. Home visits to students and their families in my Washington Heights neighborhood and Highbridge and other neighborhoods in the South Bronx and West Bronx further solidified my relationship with and understanding of my students' communities and life-worlds over time. In the early days of ELLIS, my students and I connected through talking about baseball (the school started out 98% Latino/a, mostly boys, and mostly Dominican), and I taught them science and helped them to improve their English skills, while they helped me become proficient in Spanish, especially the Dominican variety, and taught me about West African tribal cultures and politics. Many of these young people would also come to teach me important life lessons about grit and perseverance straight through incredible obstacles.

During my second year of teaching, I started writing and performing covers of popular hip-hop songs as review tools before unit exams for my chemistry classes at ELLIS. I did not know much about hip-hop's history, and its components beyond the music, or the fact that it was a movement, but I had started listening to Eminem and Kanye in college, and I enjoyed a lot of the music and found it empowering, especially when I or the students with whom I was working were "underdogs" in some way. It was only later that I would come to understand that part hip-hop's very rested in its potentially emancipatory nature.

At first, performing my chemistry raps was just fun, including mnemonic devices to help students remember key scientific facts and concepts, to review important academic vocabulary and practice English listening skills (very important for ELLs), and it also seemed to excite the students. Developing the raps became part of the routine, with a rap performance (generally a few times, with students eventually singing along and sometimes filling in missing lyrics on sheets that could then be used to review for exams) coming as they finished the unit project and right before the unit exam. Sometimes, students would beat-box or dance along as well with the song.

The following fall, I met Christopher Emdin, who had a part-time gig as science instructional coach at my school and had decided to sit in my science classroom during a couple of my classes. He seemed very enthusiastic of my approach to teaching and relating to my students, and one day he started talking about this new approach to urban science teaching with its own educational jargon, like cogenerative dialogues, cosmopolitanism and reality pedagogy. I didn't really "get" some of it the first time he showed me the slides, but we kept talking, and eventually it became apparent that I was employing nearly all of the methods for which Chris's approach advocated, just without naming them as such or realizing at first that they were connected to a culture of hip hop, a movement that I would learn started on a Sedgwick Avenue block within a couple miles from where I work and from where I live. Perhaps my favorite part of teaching was the sometimes-tangential storytelling to connect concepts to the real world (or my own research experiences or those of my friends), the discussions with students about the material as well as their lives, and working to improve my "craft" in response to students' suggestions for making the class better at meeting their needs.

From working with Chris and becoming a student as well as a practitioner of urban education, I realized that whether in teaching or in my subsequent college access work, these types of conversations were "cogens," or cogenerative dialogues. Value was placed on student voice, and students' own funds of knowledge and ways of being and expressing themselves, and I became more cognizant over time about the centrality of these types of experiences in my classroom, and then my college office, especially as I came to better understand how crucial they were to my forming strong ties with students and to my educational world-view, with its focus on hip-hop based reality pedagogy. I further realized that these cogens were in many ways analogous to hip-hop ciphers, including those that would break out spontaneously amongst students at my school while waiting outside during fire drills.

I have always been open with students about my hopes that they would pursue science, and that science offers them a "golden ticket" for helping themselves and their communities, and the world at large. As a teacher, I assigned more homework than other teachers and generally had only 2–3 students meet my expectations at any one time, but I think that may have been for the best. I would stay with students after school, sometimes past 7:00 PM, providing an environment for them to successfully complete their work, and a comfortable space for us to talk about science, their futures and ambitions, challenges they faced, and more. I also wanted the classroom space to be a comfortable and functional one, so I put a sofa in the back of the room, and my students and I converted wall, ceiling, and even table space to blackboard and whiteboard space. These spaces, which were painted by my students, were used for everything from posting assignments or setting the stage for a project to outlets for student self-expression, such as the ceiling blackboard that students would "tag" with their names or nicknames, another means of bridging between context and content in the classroom by means of valuing forms of <u>neoindigenous</u> expression.

I may have been trained as a chemist, but it was intuitive to me that connecting with students beyond the classroom and the state standards for chemistry was crucial to motivating them, that connecting the material to their lives and capitalizing on their prior knowledge was necessary, as was utilizing their strengths and leadership skills as classroom captains, whether as TAs or regulators of classroom culture or organization. Other people did not even see my students as high school material, and other students with similar educational backgrounds who were in high school generally never took a college-prep chemistry class. All of that was at the forefront of my mind in my daily fight to expand and level the chemistry playing field. Moving into advising and counseling students, and bringing paid science internships and other outside-of-class programs to these students was a no-brainer as I saw no choice but to work against a status quo that did not view my students as 4-year college contenders, let alone legitimate contenders in STEM fields with an oft-exclusionary culture. It is true that a lot of my students were far behind and did not learn science to the extent that would allow them to compete in the subject in college, but nearly all completed CSI-style investigations and a policy memo research project in response to water contamination research questions that they developed, often in light of their funds of knowledge from their own upbringings in their home countries.

Throughout my life, I have not been never very vocal about political issues, outside of engaging friends at my dinner table about issues explicitly related to educational equity. I always took a card from my mother's playbook of taking care of your work and effecting positive change, striving to become a model of effecting such change, but without making big, bold statements or attracting a ton of attention to yourself or getting involved in massive political operations or movements. I mention this because on the surface, this seems to conflict with the style of hip-hop, and that of hip-hop's outspoken nature in general. What I learned over time, however, was that my approach to working with students, as detailed above, was all about the kinds of working against the status quo, and empowerment of marginalized individuals, that hip-hop at its true roots is generally all about. Moreover, I learned about the key "knowledge of self" component within hip-hop, and my approach has definitely been all about using and fusing my understanding of my own identity, and those of my students, to help launch them into excitement about and success in science, even if on paper or to passersby they do not look like legitimate STEM contenders.

Over time, I even started including some verses about the inequalities faced by my students, such as in my "DNA" song about the genetic revolution, and my most lyrically skills song (maybe the only one with lyrical quality comparable to what my students could put together in their native languages) is a heart-felt cover about improving the world by embracing new energy technologies and helping the public to understand how alternative energies work. Nearly five years ago, I started coaching students in the inaugural year of the *Science Genius B.A.T.T.L.E.S.* program, following GZA's keynote to kick off the program, a demonstration of the unique brilliance of a hip-hop mind who I believe can make any topic sound poetic and downright fascinating. My friend Supa Swan, a local Dominican-American amateur hip-hop artist to whom I passed the torch of taking my students' lyrics – and my ability to battle with them – to a new level, also coached me on improving my own delivery as an MC and finding my voice as a person invested in hip-hop while not improperly appropriating any aspects of his culture or those of my students. In working with Chris at Columbia and delving into the study of hip-hop in conversations with hip-hop "encyclopedia" Tim Jones, I further internalized and cemented my way of working with my students as, in fact, quite aligned with hip-hop, through the lens of Chris's powerful theory of reality pedagogy. More than that, I also became a bit of student of the music and its surrounding music and cultural elements (in their more distilled forms, not the forms that often show in songs that "make it" with mass media support while glorifying misogyny and violence). As someone who focuses so much on understanding the contexts of students' lives as a pretext for connecting with and advising or mentoring them, I saw in hip-hop a vehicle for expression, connection, and for building further bridges with my students, whether on a personal or academic note or in co-constructing new emancipatory narratives with them of what they want their futures and those of their communities to look like.

My foremost passion of connecting with students and talking with them outside of the class period led to cogenerative dialogues, as I mentioned before, and ultimately to a shift in my work wherein I now spend my days focusing on advising my students and improving their "long game" of postsecondary success (in general, and in STEM for those so inclined). The different types of classroom captains that I used to utilize in my classroom further student learning and the creation of a more comfortable and culturally relevant learning space were analogous to co-teaching and the everyone-has-a-place sensibility of cosmopolitanism. Even my development and use of classroom games fell into place as part of the competition that is inherent within hip-hop culture. I am not confrontational or particularly artistic or spontaneous, but when it comes to defending and advocating for my students in the face of programs and institutions who doubt them or view them as too great a risk, I offer up a piece of my mind – backed up with evidence and, often, empirical data, since I was trained as a chemist, after all. Striving to make my students into contenders and competitors with those from more advantaged backgrounds and who had entered high school with more formal content knowledge and language skills – the vast majority of America – became a key part of my raison d'etre. I made my first (semi)-professional chemistry hip-hop music video under the direction of a former ELLIS student, with appearances from friends who are now well on their way to becoming science and health care professionals, despite a barrage of academic, socioeconomic, and linguistic challenges upon their arrival and even graduation from ELLIS. More than any of my musical projects, however, my emancipatory, transformative aim – while focusing on complex conceptual understandings that have not seen much airtime (which should change with GZA's *Dark Matter* album) – is a crucial part of the knowledge that I have of myself, and together, it makes me hip-hop.

CHAPTER 12

In Search of Power and Identity: A Hip-hop Autobiography

Lauren Leigh Kelly
@djdutchesss

This chapter was inspired by a discussion that occurred one night in Christopher Emdin's Hip-hop and Cultural Studies class a few years ago. That evening, one of my classmates presented to us the video of Queen Latifah's song, "U.N.I.T.Y.," in which Latifah speaks directly to the young, female hip-hop audience members who emulate the "ideal" romantic partner described in Apache's song, "Gangsta Bitch." Latifah raps, "You wear a rag around your head and you call yourself a 'Gangsta bitch' now that you saw Apache's video" (Latifah, 1993, track 12). In order to better understand this statement, we watched Apache's video, in which he expresses his desire for a "ghetto girl" who "don't sleep and she don't play/Stickin up girls from around the f*#kin way/Strapped but lovable, hateful but huggable/Always in trouble and definitely f*#kable" (Apache, 1993, track 4). Latifah's decision to directly address the females of the hip-hop community in this example speaks to the reality that hip-hop youth, including Black females, often construct their identities through hip-hop music and culture, and that this identity, when unchallenged, can be destructive.

As a Black female who spent much of her life constructing her identity through hip-hop, I can personally attest to this reality. Through the example of my own hip-hop autobiography, this chapter exemplifies an individual's personal and social development through hip-hop culture. For educators, the significance of hip-hop identity construction lies in the daily social reality of youth and in the critical engagement of hip-hop in an educational setting. When young people are provided with the space to deconstruct and discuss hip-hop music and culture, they can begin to truly explore their individual and social identities while also opening up space to create new possibilities of identity formation (Hill, 2009).

1   My Hip-hop Identity

I came into hip-hop as many younger siblings did – through my older brother. As a child, my admiration of Brian was immeasurable. Four years his junior,

I attempted to dress like him, be friends with his friends, and listen to everything that he did. It wasn't just the gigantic boombox that Brian brought onto the school bus in the mornings, or the baggy jeans that we both wore sagging below our boxer shorts; it wasn't simply his vigorous attempt at breakdancing or unfortunate attempt at beat mixing with cassettes. It was everything. We lived hip-hop.

In the early years, my hip-hop was simple. It told me that "parents just don't understand" which, let's be honest – they didn't. It was Busta Rhymes's verse on "Scenario" and "A room full of teachers, parents and preachers. A principal and one kid dressed in sneakers" (Leaders of the New School, 1991, track 2). I knew very little about the history and evolution of hip-hop music and culture; I simply knew that it felt good. In discovering hip-hop, something changed for me. The pop and rock music that I had listened to before was great, but it had nothing to do with me. I didn't connect to it any real or personal way. Whether or not it explicitly claimed to be, hip-hop was about me and my community. This was important for me, as a young female of color in a society dominated by White, Eurocentric culture. Finally, there was a popular culture that validated me and my dark skin. And while hip-hop had yet to reach the mainstream masses, at least I knew that I was a part of something significant and beautiful.

It was through hip-hop that my identity was shaped and developed. As an adolescent, hip-hop was how I spoke and dressed. It was wearing Mecca and Karl Kani. It was saying "mad" and "type," as in – "he was acting type stupid last night." In the 1997 documentary Rhyme & Reason, Catastraphe of the Alkaholics states that, "Everything we do [is hip-hop]. I don't give a f#%* what it is – I'm a put a hip-hop twist on it" (Sollinger & Spirer, 1997). In the philosophy of KRS-One, I was not "doing" hip-hop, I was hip-hop.

As I matured within this hip-hop world, I constructed my identity accordingly, based on what I saw of the Black females' images in the media. How purposeful or unconscious this construction was, I have yet to determine. What I do know is that when the girls in the videos wore hoodies and baggy jeans, so did I. When they wore midriff tops and "Hot Fudge" lipstick, so did I. When they had a strip of hair framing their faces on each side ... so did I. And I did so unquestioningly. Through my consumption of hip-hop music and culture, I had constructed an identity for myself that was not only false, but was also dangerous, as I sometimes presented myself as a sexualized being in ways that I did not even understand. In the words of Eisa Nefertari Ulen (2007), "These are the girls I worry about" (p. 141).

As overt feminism was a value lacking in hip-hop music and culture, it was not a part of my hip-hop identity. I did not question the cultural exploitation or objectification of females that I encountered both in music and in the hallways of my high school. When the Black male students lined the main hallway between classes to ogle and discuss the females who passed by, nothing seemed out of place. After all, that is what they did in hip-hop videos. When the males cheated on their girlfriends and the girlfriends took them back, that too was normalized. After all, the most dominant female voices in hip-hop culture existed in R&B, and a recurring theme in female R&B songs is that of forgiveness of male partners and vengeance against the "other woman." For evidence of this, see "He's Mine" by Mokenstef (1995, track 4); "The Boy is Mine," by Brandy and Monica (1998, track 2), and "Don't Mess with My Man," by Nivea (2002, track 3). In fact, music aside, looking at Black culture alone, one can find a similar trend of female acceptance of a man's infidelity or abuse (Moore, 2012; Langhorne Folan, 2010). Needless to say, I was no adolescent feminist. I accepted the role ascribed to me by my race, gender, and membership in the hip-hop community, and I feared the consequence of leaving more than I feared the effects of my subjugation. For, without hip-hop, what else was there?

I am certain that a part of me always knew that there was something wrong with the hypersexualized images of scantily-clad females in hip-hop videos and on album covers, and the translation of these representations into my reality. It was no mere coincidence that young Black males at my school felt comfortable casually touching young, Black girls' butts in the hallways. Nor was it a coincidence that most of these females simply giggled or walked away wordlessly in response. But confronting these issues also meant confronting my culture and community, which is not something that Black females are encouraged to do (Pough, 2004).

Hip-hop and I finally broke up in 1998. It was during the post-Biggie and Pac years in which rappers scrambled to be the next "King" of hip-hop, and suburban, White teens began to discover what I had always known about my culture. White girls were requesting DMX and Beenie Man at Sweet Sixteens, and suddenly, *my* White friends were testing *me* on my hip-hop knowledge. It was now trivia to them. It had been a way of life for me. But it had changed, and I refused to change with it. In those years, I felt disconnected from hip-hop. It no longer spoke to me. In fact, I barely knew what it was saying at all. I knew nothing about the so-called "underground" hip-hop movement. No one told me that my feelings were valid, or that there were other places to go to satisfy my hip-hop needs. I felt that hip-hop was no longer mine. And with the chorus of the most popular song on the radio asking, "What What What What What What What" (Noreaga, 1998, track 13). I knew it was time for me to leave.

Unfortunately, leaving the realm of hip-hop music concomitantly felt like leaving the Black community. It was a tumultuous time period for my identity. I was the only Black girl (or person) at local rock shows. The only one who looked like me at the Green Day or Ani Difranco concerts. Somehow, I had become an anomaly. As clothing grew tighter in hip-hop, mine remained baggy.

I turned to emo, alternative, and folk music. I needed something – anything that felt real. In taking a step back from hip-hop, I began to critique it for the first time. I began to think about the ways in which I had allowed hip-hop to define and shape me. I considered the actions and fashion choices that were dictated by a culture I had never before thought to question. During this time period, I learned about Nike's involvement in sweatshops, and decided to stop wearing them. One day, my boyfriend's family clowned me mercilessly for wearing New Balance sneakers, and the next day he bought me a brand new pair of Nike's. He was embarrassed by me and my unwillingness to follow the rules of hip-hop culture. I struggled in those days to choose between my own consciousness and my acceptance in the hip-hop community. And though it asked me for very little…to be a forgiving partner; wear Nike's; ignore the way in which you are exploited in music and culture; hide your intelligence; this was too much for me to negotiate. I could no longer stand passively by and allow myself to be defined by a culture that now only marginally represented me.

2   Last Night a DJ Saved My Life

In college, hip-hop and I were reunited. It was not a *dj* who "saved my life" or Napster, but rather my freshman year dorm-mate, Masai. My friend and I had just purchased cd burners, and quickly decided that it had not been a worthwhile investment. However, before I returned the device to the store, I reasoned, I should at least get some use out of it. Masai was a music collector, of sorts, and had a massive cd collection containing albums and artists that I had never heard of. I filled nearly an entire cd book with classics such as Reflection Eternal, Dead Prez, and Dilated Peoples. When I heard these artists for the first time, I was transformed. I felt as though this music was speaking to my soul. It understood me in a way that the hip-hop of my adolescence had never even tried. I had fallen back in love and realized that hip-hop did, indeed, love me in return.

I had never planned to become a dj. Rather, it was a calling…similar to how one may realize she must become a preschool teacher or join the nunnery. It was not so much a choice, but an obligation. While I had abandoned the radio and regained control over what music I listened to and what messages I internalized, I was still subject to the selections of the dj at parties and dances. This was problematic for me, as the majority of mainstream hip-hop, reggae, and even some R&B music at the time expressed moral and social values that were incongruent with my own. This occurred during the era in which Ja Rule reigned the airwaves and everyone wanted to pretend that they were from the south by slipping "herre" and "therre" into their sentences whenever possible. Young women strolled through parties with their g strings intentionally visible above the top of their Apple Bottom jeans, screaming, "I am getting so hot. I wanna take my clothes off" (Nelly, 2002, track 3). And I was sad for humanity.

The song "Chi Chi Mon" by T.O.K was popular at this time. In full disclosure, I must shamefully admit that even as a child of Jamaican parents, my understanding of *patois* is less than fluent. Hence, it was news to me when a friend one day asked, "You know this song is about burning gay people, right?" A quick revisiting of the song showed me that my friend was not only correct, but that there was no attempt made to encrypt the intent of the song. A line from the chorus states, "From dem a par inna chi chi man[1] car/ Blaze di fire mek we bun dem" (T.O.K., 2001, track 3). Translation: "Because they are riding around in gay men's cars let's shoot and kill them." I was mortified. How many times had I found myself at a party dancing and singing along to this song? When I next heard the song played at a party, I froze in place. I did not want to move, for fear that this would make me complicit in the violent content of the song. I watched the bodies around me, dancing, swaying, singing along to a song that proudly promoted the hatred and murder of homosexuals. It made me ill. While this song is an extreme example, as it is reflective of a particular section of Jamaican culture that vilifies homosexuality, it is indicative of the extent to which young people can unwittingly support intolerance and real or imagined violence against any practice that falls outside of what is acceptable in mainstream culture. In his song "Black Zombies," Nas raps, "Walkin' talkin' dead, though we think we're livin'; We just copy-cat, followin' the system" (2002, track 10). There is something zombie-like about turning off one's brain and simply moving his body to the tune of someone else's whim.

I grew tired of going to parties whose dj's implicitly asked me to either ignore the offensive content of the songs he played so that I could partake in the revelry, or stand in the corner, miserable, waiting for a Missy Elliot song to come on. Even those dj's who condemned the misogyny and materialism of mainstream hip-hop music failed me at parties by playing super-"conscious" hip-hop that is more appropriate for sitting in a dorm room with "revolutionary" friends, plotting how to take down "The Man," than for dancing. Hearing these songs at parties simply reminded me of my historical oppression and how problematic it was to be at a college party while my people were out there suffering. Unwilling to forsake my penchant for dancing or my own values, I realized what I had to do. Clearly, a balance had to be struck between these two extremes. Someone needed to play music that people could dance to without condoning the oppression of women, homosexuality, or consciousness. And since no one else was stepping up, I realized that this person had to be me. By gaining power over the media that I consumed and shared, I had found a space for resistance to dominant ideas and representations, while, as one of few female *dj*'s at the time, I was able to imagine and create new representations of identity.

3   Hip-hop Education

I became an educator for many of the same reasons that led me to *djing*. It was a natural progression. Because hip-hop was an integral part of my identity, it was an intrinsic part of my teaching. As an English teacher, it made sense to me to bring hip-hop into the classroom for student engagement, literary analysis, and critical discourse. However, with English content as the primary focus of my classroom instruction, it was difficult to find space for in-depth study of hip-hop texts. As a result, inclusion of hip-hop literature in my class was marginal. While I noticed that students were fully engaged in lessons that dealt with hip-hop, there was little room in the curriculum to explore the connections between hip-hop and identity, culture, representation, and power.

As our society becomes increasingly saturated with media, it is even more vital to critically examine media in the classroom (Parmar, 2006). Critical hip-hop literacy is a powerful way to support students in gaining control over their media consumption and hip-hop identities (Kelly, 2015). Since the high school English curriculum that I followed lacked the space for extensive instruction in Critical hip-hop literacy, I created and taught a half-year, English elective class called Hip-hop Literature and Culture in the high school in which I have worked for many years. The class utilizes hip-hop texts and media (lyrics, music videos, documentaries, memoirs, literary criticisms, etc.) as a means to foster critical conversations about youth culture, media consumption, and individual and social identity.

I once attended a birthday party thrown by a two-time college graduate. Most of the attendees at this party were mid-twenties, formally educated, professional people of color. At one point during this event, someone requested that the Two Chainz "Birthday Song" be played. When the song came on, the party attendees grew animated and ecstatic. Arms were thrown up in the air, and nearly every voice – male and female – came together to shout out the chorus, "All I want for my birthday is a big booty ho!" (2012, track 5). As I stood there, frozen and dumbfounded, my mind flashed back to a previous moment that had occurred in class in which my students insisted that we watch the video for this very song. I reluctantly agreed, and was immediately uncomfortable. The video follows the rapper Two Chainz around a birthday party at a house that is replete with underdressed females, one of whom is laying on the dining room table, covered in icing. Similar to Apache's "Gangsta Bitch," this song puts forth particular representations of masculinity and femininity through the images of "desirable" females who males want to possess and who females aspire to be. My concern is not that such songs and videos exist, but rather that they often exist unchallenged and not critiqued by its consumers.

Media consumers often construct their ideas of what it means to be Black and what it means to be hip-hop based on what they hear and see in the music and media representations. (Jeffries, 2007). If these representations go unquestioned, one can easily find herself in a room full of men and women of color who have no qualms about belting out their desires, (real or imagined) for a "big-booty ho." If this is the case for adults, then what does that mean for our adolescent students who are immersed in hip-hop culture? The problem with keeping hip-hop out of education is that it limits the possibilities for critical engagement of popular media with the young people who most consume this media (Parmar, 2006; Kirkland, 2007).

The danger in this is not that consumers receive ideas based on popular culture, but rather that few popular alternatives exist when it comes to cultural representations in media (Kellner & Share, 2007; Rose, 2003). Without the space to examine these representations and construct new ones, young consumers of popular culture run the risk of emulating the very identity representations that exploit and limit them (Kellner & Share, 2005). Hip-hop education is not simply about bringing hip-hop into the classroom for student engagement, or about celebrating hip-hop through academic study. While these are both facets of hip-hop education, and should continue as a part of hip-hop pedagogy, the underlying purpose of hip-hop education is to provide a space for critical engagement with popular texts and cultural representations, and to support students in examining and constructing social, cultural, and individual identities.

Note

1   Derogatory term for homosexual in Jamaican patois.

References

2 Chainz. (2012). Birthday song. On *Based on a T.R.U. story* [Digital Download]. New York, NY: Def Jam.
Apache. (1992). Gangsta bitch. On *Apache ain't shit* [CD]. New York, NY: Tommy Boy.
Hill, M. L. (2001). *Beats rhymes & classroom life*. New York, NY: Teachers College Press.
Jeffries, M. (2007). Re: Definitions: The name and game of hip-hop feminism. In A. Durham, G. Pough, R. Raimist, & E. Richardson (Eds.), *Home girls make some noise: Hip-hop feminism anthology* (pp. 208–227). Mira Loma, CA: Parker Publishing, LLC.

Kellner, D., & Share, J. (2005). Toward critical media literacy: Core concepts, debates, organizations, and policy. *Discourse: Studies in the Cultural Politics of Education, 26*(3), 369–386.

Kellner, D., & Share, J. (2007). Critical media literacy, democracy, and the reconstruction of education. In D. Macedo & S. R. Steinberg (Eds.), *Media literacy: A reader* (pp. 3–23). New York, NY: Peter Lang Publishing.

Kelly, L. L. (2015). You don't have to claim her: Reconstructing Black femininity through critical hip-hop literacy. *Journal of Adolescent & Adult Literacy, 59*(5), 529–538.

Kirkland, D. (2007). Foreword. In M. Diaz & M. Runell (Eds.), *The hip-hop education guidebook* (Vol. 1, pp. 11–12). New York, NY: Hip-Hop Association Inc.

Langhorne Folan, K. (2010). *Don't bring home a White boy.* New York, NY: Karen Hunter Publishing.

Latifah, Q. (1993). U.N.I.T.Y. On *Black reign* [CD]. New York, NY: Motown Records.

Leaders of the New School. (1991). Case of the P.T.A. On *A future without a past...* [Vinyl]. New York, NY: Elektra.

Mokenstef. (1995). He's mine. On *Azz izz* [CD]. New York, NY: Def Jam.

Monica & Norwood, B. (1998). The boy is mine. On *Never say never and the boy is mine* [CD]. Los Angeles, CA: Atantic & Arista.

Moore, D. J. (2012). *The relationship between ethnicity, ethnic identity, and tolerance of infidelity among college women at risk for HIV* (Doctoral dissertation). Ohio State University, Columbus, OH. Retrieved from http://etd.ohiolink.edu/send-pdf.cgi/Moore%20Dana%20Jenae.pdf?osu1338086135

Nas. (2002). Black zombie. On *The Lost tapes* [CD]. New York, NY: Columbia.

Nelly. (2002). Hot in herre. On *Nellyville* [CD]. New York, NY: Universal.

Nivea. (2002). Don't mess with my man. On *Nivea* [CD]. New York, NY: Jive.

Noreaga. (1998). Superthug. On *N.O.R.E.* [Vinyl]. New York, NY: Tommy Boy.

Parmar, P. (2006). The power of rap as a form of literacy. In S. R. Steinberg (Ed.), *Contemporary youth culture: An international encyclopedia* (pp. 527–530). Westport, CT: Greenwood Press.

Pough, G. D. (2004). *Check it while I wreck it: Black womanhood, hip-hop culture, and the public sphere.* Boston, MA: Northeastern University Press.

Rose, T. (2003, March 1). Race, sex, and stigmas. *New York Times*, p. A19.

Sollinger, D. (Producer), & Spirer, P. (Director). (1997). *Rhyme & reason* [Motion picture]. United States: Miramax.

T.O.K. (2001). Chi chi man. On *My crew, my dawgs* [Vinyl]. New York, NY: VP Records.

Ulen, E. N. (2007). They're not talking about me. In A. Durham, G. Pough, R. Raimist, & E. Richardson (Eds.), *Home girls make some noise: Hip-hop feminism anthology* (pp. 141–147). Mira Loma, CA: Parker Publishing, LLC.

PART 4

Addressing Mental Health through Hip-hop Education

∵

Tweets

 Ian Levy EdD
@IanPLevy

Freud speaks of "Free-association", or
having clients write freely to unearth
emotion. Freestyle is no different
#HipHopEd

 E!
@etheemcee

It's all about introducing new ways to cope.
Instead of drinking or smoking, tell em' 2
write whatever's on their mind #HipHopEd

 Lauren Leigh Kelly
@djdutchesss

I don't know how to get crack out the ghetto
or stop racial profiling. Except to talk about
it. #HipHopEd

 A. Harmony
@AHarmonyMusic

Hip hop helps so many people
process/articulate emotions they may not
even understand. Or aren't willing to
address otherwise. #HipHopEd

 Cee O.
@@NoLimits224

Kendrick Lamar's "u" paints a vivid pic. of
how trauma in one's childhood when not
addressed can lead to emotional distress.
#HipHopEd

Introduction to Part 4: Addressing Mental Health through Hip-hop Education

Christopher Emdin and Ian P. Levy
@ChrisEmdin and @IanPLevy

> My family customs were not accustomed to dealing with mental health/
> It was more or less an issue for white families with wealth/
> Void, I defected, employed. self annoyed/
> Went independent, enjoyed stealth
> PHAROAHE MONCH

The above quote is from a song by rapper Pharoahe Monch, where he discusses the complex relationship between urban youth of color and mental health. His lyrics describe the tensions between urban youth family/traditions and seeking mental health. In many ways, it exemplifies the conditions of many young people of color who are deeply entrenched in a form of expression like hip-hop, yet unable to fully express themselves in ways that allow them to grow mentally and academically. Pharoahe also alludes to the general misperception that addressing one's mental health concerns is a practice only for white socioeconomically advantaged populations – *"My family customs were not accustomed to dealing with mental health. It was more or less an issue for white families with wealth."* In this lyric Pharoahe speaks to the realities of young people of color who often come from urban environments where they are significantly less likely to be provided with mental health care in comparison with White youth (Holm-Hansen, 2006). Building on Pharoahe's point, even when care is provided, disparities are present in the quality and complexity of those services (Holm-Hansen, 2006). In this part, Cassandra Ogbevire brilliantly describes the landscape of these inequities, and how Pharoahe's feelings toward mental health, echo those of young people she works with. As Pharoahe describes choosing to go *"independent"* rather than procure services, he describes the experiences of students like Tee that Ogbevire introduces to the reader and mirrors data which suggests that men's willingness to seek counseling is quite low, most likely due to the label of being perceived as vulnerable and weak in the context of socialized male gender norms (Andrews, Issakidis, & Carter, 2001; Husaini, Moore, & Cain, 1994; McKay, Rutherford, Cacciola, & Kabasakalian-McKay, 1996; O'Neil, Good, & Holmes, 1995; Thom, 1986; Wills & DePaulo, 1991). However, this urge to be perceived as

© KONINKLIJKE BRILL NV, LEIDEN, 2018 | DOI 10.1163/9789004371873_017

strong/inexpressive does not mean that young men of color are unable to express themselves. Rather, it is the process that even though men are aware of their emotion, they choose not to express them in the context of evaluations for the emotion's causes, modes, and consequences (Wong & Rochlen, 2005).

Consequently, men like Pharoahe who *"went independent"* and *"enjoyed stealth,"* have likely been conditioned to discourage from feeling negative emotions such as sadness and fear that may attribute to label of vulnerability and weakness stemming from gender differences in emotional regulation and expression (Blazina & Marks, 2001; Cusack, Deane, Wilson, & Ciarrochi, 2006; Kashdan, Mishra, Breen, & Froh, 2009; Nolen-Hoeksema & Aldao, 2011). Furthermore, they are more likely to make poor decisions that affirm stereotypes about who they are. In many cases, urban youth will self-medicate by using substances like alcohol and/or marijuana in order to mask emotions and uphold masculine images (Mason & Korpela, 2008). Melvin Williams describes this process in his chapter, and examines how identity construction around alcohol consumption can be deconstructed through hip-hop.

Pharoahe Monch's words also outline the general responses that urban youth of color have to personal challenges (deflection, hyperindependence) that would/could otherwise be addressed by school personnel who are equipped to help them work through potential mental health issues. This is important because the academic achievement of African American and Latino/a youth who populate urban schools has been reported to fall far below that of their counterparts from other ethnic and socioeconomic backgrounds (NCES, 2006). However, traditional structures within urban schools inundate school counselors with administrative assignments that eventually strip them of their ability to work with students in times of need (Paisely & Borders, 1995). This reality strengthens an already existing mistrust of school counselors, and mental health services overall, because students are told to visit their school counselor in times of distress, and find that they are not available to assist them. In fact, even when counselors are available, they are commonly instructed to utilize reactive, "band-aid," approaches to counseling which focus on addressing student issues on a surface level and getting them back to class as quickly as possible (Paisely & Borders, 1995). This furthers youth alienation from seeking mental health services, and ultimately positions students emotional needs in competition with "seat-time" (time students spend in a seat in a classrooms).

Consequently, within this book part we not only cover the pedagogy implications of #HipHopEd, but also, we argue that the nature of youth responses to mental health concerns is an under-focused dimension of teaching and learning, and has a deleterious effect on academic achievement. Raphael Travis and Joshua Childs take on this issue in their chapter on the role of social workers in the #HipHopEd movement. They argue that if the youth who traditionally underperform in schools are also the ones who are least likely to seek therapy, and come from communities where mental health stressors are most prevalent, it is imperative that we consider a how to best integrate culturally responsive mental health practices into urban schools. Furthermore, they outline such a model through a description of Empowerment-based Positive Youth Development (EMPYD) and the way it informs what they describe as a hip-hop based Individual and Community Empowerment (ICE) framework. This part concludes with a chapter by Ian Levy's chapter, he discusses an addition model for hip-hop therapy based group counseling model that may be utilized by school counselors and/or mental health counseling professional. Pulling from previously established group counseling theory, this final chapter showcases the power and value of the hip hop cypher in creating the space necessary for group counseling services to be deployed.

In this part we interrogate the effectiveness of a hip-hop based therapies that seek to address academic and health based disparities for young people in urban schools. Specifically it will cover: (1) the implications hip-hop culture has on perceptions of mental health, (2) the role pedagogy play in addressing substance abuse issues amongst urban youth, (3) hip-hop therapy as a group counseling framework, and (4) the role social workers play in school #HipHopEd more broadly. These approaches are seen as crucial in helping young people overcome the emotional barriers that hinder academic performance.

References

NCES. (2006). *The health literacy of America's adults: Results from the 2003 National Assessment of Adult Literacy* (NCES 2006–483). Washington, DC: National Center for Education Statistics.

Paisley, P. O., & Borders, L. D. (1995). School counseling: An evolving specialty. *Journal of Counseling & Development, 74*(2), 150–153.

CHAPTER 13

Hop Saved My Life: Addressing Mental Health Needs and Suicide Rates of African American Male Youth

Cassandra Ogbevire
@NoLimits224

Mental Illness. The phrase itself evokes emotions ranging from disgust to empathy based on an individual's familiarity with it. According to the National Alliance of Mental Illness (NAMI), mental illness is defined as a, "medical condition that disrupts a person's thinking, feeling, mood, ability to relate to others and daily functioning" ("What Is Mental Illness?" Fact Sheet, 2013). Despite mental illness being considered a medical condition similar to Diabetes and Hypertension (Reeves et al., 2011); it is highly stigmatized in our global community because of fear and lack of knowledge (SAMHSA Mental Health Info Center, 2003). Stigma related to mental illness has resulted in the development of barriers that negatively impact the quality of life for individuals suffering with a mental illness (Corrigan & Watson, 2002).

Many Americans are affected by mental illness and its rising prevalence has become a public health issue. A 2011 report by The Center for Disease Control Prevention state at least 50% of United States will develop at least one mental disorder during his or her lifetime (Reeves et al., 2011). Many individuals that suffer from mental illness are more likely to experience low self-esteem and have difficulty maintaining employment and social relationships (Corrigan & Watson, 2002). Without treatment, mental illness can lead to the following challenges: substance abuse, disability, unemployment, homelessness, incarceration, and more alarming – suicide. Undertreated mental illness can eventually lead to the development of severe mental illnesses such as, Schizophrenia, Major Depression, or Bipolar Disorder. As a result of severe mental illness, America loses $193.2 billion per year in earnings (NAMI "What is Mental Illness Fact Sheet?" 2013). Since many individuals with severe mental illness isolate themselves and experience a diminished capacity to cope with the demands of life, many of these individuals are unable to keep consistent employment.

Despite these alarming statistics, prevalence of mental illness is rising due to misdiagnosis and underestimation in our country. Prevalence estimates of mental illness vary due to a number of reasons. The diagnosis of mental illness is based on criteria found in the American Psychiatric Association's Diagnostic and Statistical Manual of Mental Disorders (DSM-IV) and a clinician's judgment. Unfortunately, many survey instruments used to capture mental illness are poorly constructed, as a result generated mental illness report do not adequately present prevalence rates of mental illness (Reeves et al., 2011). Other factors that contribute to the inconsistencies of mental illness prevalence are supported by the onset delay of symptoms and engagement in mental health treatment. Typical onset of mental illness symptoms occurs during adolescence, but many adolescents become very ambivalent about engaging in mental health services (Lindsey, Joe, & Nebbitt, 2010). On average the most frequent delay across different mental illness symptoms is a decade and the longest delays can persist for about 20 years (Reeves et al., 2011). Ambivalence towards mental health treatment is attributed to poor mental health literacy and psychosocial barriers. The literature suggests under-treatment or no treatment of mental illness leads to a more severe mental illness that is difficult to treat (Lindsey, Joe, & Nebbitt, 2010; Watkins, Walker, & Griffin, 2010).

Long-term effects of not addressing mental illness are detrimental to our country financially and socially. Delays of treating mental illness lead to severe disability and other adverse health outcomes that result in higher healthcare costs). Secondly, rates for both intentional and unintentional injuries are increased among people with a mental illness (NAMI, ibid) According to the CDC (2011), people with mental illness are 2 to 6 times more likely to experience intentional (i.e. homicide and suicide) and unintentional (i.e. motor vehicles) injuries compared to the general public. Despite the increased prevalence of mental illness, those who experience mental illness are inappropriately served and become consistently ostracized in our community. Therefore, it is imperative for healthcare systems to incorporate appropriate and effective mental health care practices to reduce costs and injuries related to untreated mental illness.

There are many barriers that hinder individuals with mental illness from receiving adequate treatment. Some factors that hinder mental illness treatment include socioeconomic status, mental health illiteracy, racial/ethnic classification, and lack of insurance (NAMI, ibid.). Similarly, to other medical conditions, there is a disparity related to mental health care usage based on racial/ethnic classification. Gulliver, Griffiths, and Christensen (2010) found racial and ethnic minorities such as Native Americans, Latino Americans, Asian Americans, Pacific Island Americans, and African Americans experience a disproportionately high burden of disability because of mental illness). For instance, stigmatizing attitudes towards mental illness is the primary factor that hinders African American adults from utilizing mental health treatment in alarming rates (Gulliver, Griffiths, & Christensen, 2010). A factor that contributes to the underutilization of mental health services for African Americans is the media's portrayal of mental illness. The media portrays those with a mental illness as unstable, deranged, and lacking self-sufficiency. These negative stereotypes of mental illness by the media invoke embarrassment and fear within African Americans struggling with a mental illness; consequently, many become leery of engaging in mental health services.

Within the past ten years, the prevalence of mental illness has risen astronomically among African American youth, particularly in African American male youth. For example, the rate of suicide for African American male youth was approximately 3 times higher than African American female youth (African American Suicide Fact Sheet, 2010). Research suggests that African American male youth are exposed to more psychosocial stressors than other racial and gender groups over their life. These factors increase their vulnerability for poorer mental health outcomes. Despite these findings, literature suggests that these increased rates of suicide are attributed to possible masked mental illnesses. Unfortunately, African American male youth are least likely to access mental health services. Factors that influence the low utilization of mental health services among African American male youth include, mistrust of the mental health provider and system, fear of being labeled "crazy," and breaching of confidentiality (Lindsey & Marcell, 2012). As a result, many African American male youth use alternative methods to cope with psychological distress. In this chapter I argue for the importance of using hip-hop culture (specifically expression) to mitigate suicide risks among African American male youth.

Perceived exposure to violence and stress increases the probability of mental illness among African American male youth. Chronic exposure to stress and violence is detrimental to an individual's well-being, specifically to their mental health status. Watkins, Walker, and Griffith (2010) found African American male youth that live in under-resourced and urban communities are more likely to have frequent exposures to violence. In fact, based on this exposure young people from urban areas may be at an increased risk of developing symptoms commonly associated with Posttraumatic Stress Disorder. Posttraumatic Stress Disorder is an anxiety disorder that is attributed to experiencing traumatic events, which can lead to denial, emotional numbing, depression, or feelings of anxiety (Hall, Cassidy, & Stevenson, 2008). Many African American male youth that develop feelings of anxiety in response to chronic stress and violence develop unhealthy coping strategies, predominantly related to substance abuse (Lindsey & Marcell, 2012).

Socialization of Black Masculinity is known to discourage the use of mental health treatment among African American male youth, even if they do experience mental illness. Many African American male youth are bombarded with contradicting images of Black manhood from the media, family members, and their local community. In general, young men are socialized to believe they are invulnerable to illness and seeking help is a sign of weakness. Unfortunately, many African American male youth are discouraged to talk about their mental illness within their communities. Consequently, African American male youth who experience depressive symptoms are more likely to isolate themselves. Compared to their counterparts, African American male youth counter fear of appearing weak and/or vulnerable by masking depressive symptoms under the guise of being tough and strong among peers (Lindsey, Joe, & Nebbit, 2010). Since African American male youth are economically and socially marginalized, they exhibit forms of masculinity detrimental to their health, such as glorifying and mimicking a "street life" persona. The combination of young African American malesexposure to chronic violence, stress, and substance abuse can exacerbate symptoms of mental illness that are left untreated.

Stigmatizing attitudes toward formal mental health services serve as a barrier for many young African American males engagement in mental health care. A bevy of research suggests African American male youth have a large amount of skepticism toward reaching out to professional mental health clinicians (Lindsey et al., 2013; Lindsey et al., 2012; Earl, Williams, & Anglade, 2011; Watkins, Walker, & Griffith, 2010). This could be because African American male youth display mistrust towards mental health clinicians, a feeling often held by African American adults as well (Alvidrez, Snowden, & Kaiser, 2008). Past mistreatments and negative outcomes of care from mental health institutions contribute to this group's current mistrust of mental health services. Many African American male youth that experience mental illness internalize negative stereotypes of mental illness from the public as their own (Lindsey & Marcell, 2012). Lindsey and Marcell (2012) found African American male youth have greater difficulty confiding to mental health clinicians, since they believe they are unable to relate or can help them assist in their mental health care.

Perceived exposure to violence, socialization of Black masculinity, and stigmatizing attitudes are the most studied factors related to young African American males'poor usage of mental health treatment found in the literature (Lindsey et al., 2013; Lindsey et al., 2012; Watkins, Walker, & Griffith, 2010). In spite of these findings, there is a dire need for interventions that are culturally competent and address the mental health needs of African American male youth. African American male youth possess the lowest expectancy of life compared to their male and female counterparts (African American Suicide Fact Sheet, 2010). Additionally, in the past twenty years, the suicide rates among this group have steadily increased rather than decrease according to recent research findings (African American Suicide Fact Sheet, 2010). Cultural and social constructs primarily discourage African American male youth to be open about their feelings and needs related to their mental well-being. Consequently, I argue for clinical and public health practices, rooted in hip-hop to help young people tackle emotions they normally would eschew. Through detailing my personal experiences working with an African American male youth with a history of mental illness at a homeless shelter in Chicago, I aim to suggest the healing power of hip-hop.

Working as a Youth Specialist at the homeless shelter in Chicago, I typically encountered young people who ranged from 14–23 years old. Many of which found themselves homeless due to experiencing instability in their homes, or being viewed as rebellious by their caretakers. The majority of the youth that resided within this homeless shelter experienced trauma, and were diagnosed with mental illnesses such as Bipolar Disorder, Major Depressive, and Schizoaffective Disorder. Being a naïve, recent college graduate at the time, I was easily intimidated by many of the youth's boisterous personalities and blunt demeanor. Especially, since I heard horror stories of the interactions of youth with new staff during moments of conflict among their peers. However, one young African American male, named Tee, always seemed to be the common denominator in many conflicts.

At the time, Tee was a 19-year-old male diagnosed with Schizoaffective Disorder ("A chronic mental health condition characterized by symptoms of schizophrenia, such as hallucinations/delusions and symptoms of a mood disorder, NAMI " Schizoaffective Disorder" Fact Sheet, 2014). He loved Spoken Word and was always found debating with staff and peers about philosophical topics. Generally, Tee avoided talking about himself. He felt much more comfortable discussing things he had read about in books. However, many times during debates or conversations, Tee was very condescending and this characteristic annoyed many other youth, leading him to become involved in many altercations with his peers.

Over time, I noticed Tee would go through manic/depressive episodes where he was easily engaged and pleasant for a few minutes, but would then easily flip to become quite irritated and angry. During his manic episodes he was passively aggressive towards staff members and his peers, which made interacting in the milieu very difficult. The only thing that calmed Tee down was being in the studio where he created beats and freestyles. Instead of asking to take his medication or scheduling an appointment to see the shelter's psychiatrist; Tee would ask to be locked in the studio. Over time, Tee began sharing his songs with me and I noticed there were filled with raw emotion and honesty about challenges he experienced. Tee was not the only young African American male suffering with mental illness who made the studio his safe haven in the shelter; many of his peers who shared similar challenges were drawn to the studio and freestyling. In the studio I saw many of the youth who isolated themselves in the milieu create a brotherhood among each other. Most importantly, I witnessed many of the youth become truthful about their situations and gained strength in their transparency and vulnerability. In many ways freestyling in the studio collectively as a group allowed the young men to engage in a collective catharsis.

The elements of freestyling in hip-hop served as a medium for youth to describe their truth without any restrictions and judgment. Through freestyling in a cypher many of the youth like Tee were empowered and pushed passed their disappointments, fears, and pains. In many ways freestyling became their outlet for stress and anger. Also, freestyling allowed the youth to become empowered in their identity. Susan Hadley and George Yancy (2012) in their book, *Therapeutic Uses of Rap and Hip-hop* go in great detail discussing the different ways hip-hop can assist in positive youth development and healing.

Many other individuals that work with urban youth have incorporated elements of hip-hop in intervention programs to improve mental health literacy among youth and reduce stigma related to engagement of mental health services. Programs like *Check Your Head – Mental Health America of Colorado and Hip-hop Psychology* abroad are particularly important for African American male youth that are experiencing mental illness. *Check Your Head Mental Health America of Colorado*, is a schoolbased program that incorporates hip-hop elements to help students learn about mental health and use creative performance to express their identities. Similarly, Hip hop Psych is a public health initiative that uses hip-hop lyrics to challenge stereotypes associated with mental health in an innovative manner. These hip-hop inspired programs meet each youth where there are and provide a familiar setting to eradicate psychosocial barriers related to engaging in mental health services. Hip-hop is not just an activity youth engage in but a culture that many African American male youth identify with daily and become empowered in.

Hip-hop has always been a rebellious force that challenges social injustices that plague urban communities. Hip-hop serves as a therapeutic medium for its artists and listeners. Unfortunately, today majority of hip-hop culture glamorizes excessive substance usage and machismo, which is detrimental to overall mental wellness in African Americans – especially for African American male youth. Despite these negative images, hip-hop in the last 20 years has begun depicting the Black Man's struggle to cope with mental illness.

Conversely, there are several hip-Hop songs that depict a Black male revealing his personal challenges with mental illness. Kid Cudi in his song, "Dr. Pill" discusses the discomfort he experiences taking prescribed antidepressants. Scarface in "Born Killer" divulges about being diagnosed with Manic Depression. DMX struggles with his self-worth due to his painful childhood in "Look Thru My Eyes." Geto Boys in their song, "Mind Playing Tricks on Me" repeatedly discuss the effects of paranoia. Gorilla Zoe in "Lost" confesses to feeling out of control due to the uncertainties of his life. Recently, Pharaohe Monch in "Losing My Mind" discloses his friends and family's lack of knowledge related to his mental illness.

In Lupe Fiasco's song, "Hip-hop Saved My Life" I am reminded of the power that manifests when one share's his or her truth. Similar to Lupe, Tee used hip-hop as a means to reconcile the discrepancy between his current situation and desired future. Hip-hop allowed Tee to confront his challenges in a manner that was deeply rooted in his strengths instead of his weaknesses. Through hip-Hop Tee's story is easily shareable within his community but most importantly among his peers.

The unfiltered narratives of mental illness in hip-hop songs give us a glimpse of pain and coping mechanisms used by those suffering with mental illness in this population. Ironically, we as a community listen attentively to misogynistic lyrics but fall deaf to the anguish of mental illness expressed in hip-hop songs. With drastic budget cuts and the increased rise of suicide among African American male youth, there has not been a more critical time for the hip-hop village to step in the forefront to save its young people. Hip-hop is our solution to educating the urban community about the truths of mental illness. Hip-hop can end the shame associated with mental illness. Hip-hop is the medium for African American male youth to freely express their struggles without backlash. Most importantly, hip-hop equips us with tools to dismantle social injustices that ail under-resourced communities. I charge the hip-hop village to break the silence and dispel myths associated with mental illness in order to save the lives of African American male youth before it's too late.

References

Alvidrez, J., Snowden, R. L., & Kaiser, M. D. (2008). The experience of stigma among Black mental health consumers. *Journal of Health Care for the Poor and Underserved, 19*(3), 874–893.

American Association of Suicidology. (2010). *African American suicide fact sheet.* Retrieved from http://www.suicidology.org/resources/suicide-fact-sheets

Corrigan, W. P., & Watson, C. A. (2002). Understanding the impact of stigma on people with mental illness. *World Psychiatry, 1*(1), 16–20.

Gulliver, A., Griffiths, M. K., & Christensen, H. (2010). Perceived barriers and facilitators to mental health help-seeking in young people: A systematic review. *BMS Psychiatry, 10*(1), 1–9.

Earl, T., Williams, D., & Anglade, S. (2011). An update on the mental health of Black Americans: Puzzling dilemmas and needed research. *Journal of Black Psychology, 37*(4), 485–498.

Hall, M. D., Cassidy, E., & Stevenson, C. H. (2008). Acting "tough" in a " tough" world: An examination of fear among urban African American adolescents. *Journal of Black Psychology, 34*, 381–389.

Handley, S., & Yancy, G. (2012). *Therapeutic uses of rap and hip-hop.* New York, NY: Taylor and Francis Group, LLC.

Lindsey, A. M., Chambers, K., Pohle, C., Beall, P., & Lucksted, A. (2013). Understanding the behavioral determinants of mental health services by urban, under-sourced Black youth: Adolescent and caregiver perspectives. *Journal of Child Family Studies, 22*, 107–121.

Lindsey, A. M., & Marcell, V. A. (2012). "We're going through a lot of struggles that people don't even know about": The need to understand African American males' help-seeking for mental health on multiple levels. *American Journal of Men's Health, 6*(5), 354–364.

Lindsey, A. M., Joe, S., & Nebbitt, V. (2010). Family matters: The role of mental health stigma and social support on depressive symptoms and subsequent help seeking among African American boys. *Journal of Black Psychology, 36*(4), 458–482.

National Alliance Mental Illness. (2013). *"Schizoaffective disorder" fact sheet.* United States: National Alliance Mental Illness.

National Alliance Mental Illness. (2013). *"What is mental illness" fact sheet.* United States: National Alliance Mental Illness.

Reeves, C. W., Strine, W. T., Pratt, A. L., Thompson, W., Ahluwalia, I., Dhingra, S. S., McKnight-Ely, R. L., Harrison, L. D., Angelo, V. D., Williams, L., Morrow, B., Gould, D., & Safran, A. M. (2011). *Mental illness surveillance among U.S. adults.* Centers for Disease Control Preventions, Office of Surveillance, Epidemiology, and Laboratory Services.

SAMHSA Mental Health Information Center. (2003). *"Anti-stigma: Do you know the facts?" fact sheet.* Washington, DC: U.S. Department of Health and Human Services.

Watkins, C. D., Walker, L. R., & Griffith, M. G. (2010). A meta-study of Black male mental health and well being. *Journal of Black Psychology, 36*(3), 303–330.

CHAPTER 14

"Turn Down for What?": A Critical Examination of Black Youth Alcohol Consumption and the Influence of Hip-hop Media

Melvin Williams
@Hiphopprofi6

1   Introduction

As a youth, I did not experience the elations commonly affiliated with a progressive social upbringing. I grew up in the 1990s, an era when the problematic relationship between the alcohol industry and hip-hop media was beginning to devastate the African American community through musical releases such as Snoop Dogg's "Gin and Juice," "Cypress Hill's "Tequila Sunrise," and Mobb Deep's "Drink Away the Pain." In my Memphis, Tennessee neighborhood, there were significantly more alcohol advertisements (often depicting hip-hop artists) than educational advertisements showcased on billboards, creating an environment where alcohol consumption was promoted over educational advancement. Additionally, alcohol consumption was a household fixture among my relatives, who battled the demon of alcohol addiction in their attempts to navigate the perils of low-income employment, motherhood and fatherhood, and unjust racial politics in the South. Based on these socioeconomic politics, hip-hop music offered them both a source of escapism and an entertainment source to support their unhealthy drinking habits.

I can vividly remember hearing hip-hop music throughout my grandmother's home and watching my loved ones ingest unhealthy amounts of alcohol, as they attempted to emulate the glorified lifestyle of a hip-hop artist. The pattern painted a distorted view of adulthood for me, and before I knew it, I too began to view alcohol use as a critical element of Black masculinity construction. Subsequently, I struggled with the demon of alcohol addiction myself as a teenager. My adoration for hip-hop culture and desire to emulate the "esteemed" lifestyles of my drunken relatives and beloved rappers had manifested into a behavior, and I found myself contributing to the growing statistic of underage, alcohol consumers in the Black community.

© KONINKLIJKE BRILL NV, LEIDEN, 2018 | DOI 10.1163/9789004371873_019

It happened quickly as I began to "come into my own as a man," filling my body with fluids that revolutionized my sentiments on adulthood, hip-hop culture, and the perils of being a Black male adolescent in a poverty-laden neighborhood. In my eyes, I was enacting the script of a hip-hop fan whose use of alcohol asserted a hyper-masculine identity of cool pose that was authentic to the musical genre I adored so dearly. In fact, it was not until I began doctoral study that I started to examine the connections between the alcohol industry, hip-hop media, and the alcohol-related health disparities facing Black youth in the United States.

In this chapter, I chapter critically analyzed hip-hop media and its influence on Black youth and alcohol consumption. Specifically, this chapter aims to expose the commodification of hip-hop by the alcohol industry and its efforts to disproportionately target Black youth. This research explores the potential of hip-hop to teach alcohol-specific media literacy to youth populations. The first two sections briefly outline the alarming rates of alcohol consumption among Black youth and the historic role of hip-hop as a form of cultural resistance for the population. The third section presented a historical account of hip-hop media's synergistic relationship with the alcohol industry. The latter part of this chapter applied the insights gained from this examination to explore potential pedagogical applications of hip-hop to teach alcohol-specific media literacy to youth populations.

2 "I Walk in, Then I Turn up!": The Problem of Black Youth Alcohol Consumption

The historic trend of showcasing hip-hop artists in alcohol marketing represents a ploy by the alcohol industry to capture the attention of Black youth, an audience that once reported lower rates of alcohol use, drunkenness, and alcohol-related problems when compared to other races (Herd, 1989). As hip-hop media are modified and used to purvey harmful consumer products to Black communities, its emancipatory potential is now being transformed into a system of domination that profits directly from negatively impacting an already poverty-stricken community. Alcohol is the most widely used drug by Black youth, with nearly 65% of Black high school students admitting to having had at least a sip of alcohol and an estimated 25% reporting initial alcohol consumption before age 13 (Eaton et al., 2012). Such early consumption is problematic for the Black youth population.

Research has shown that young people who begin drinking before age 15 are four times more likely to develop alcohol dependence than those who wait until age 21 to become drinkers (Grant & Dawson, 1997). African

Americans suffer more from alcohol-related diseases than other groups in the US population. The age-adjusted death rate from alcohol-related diseases for non-Hispanic African Americans is 31% greater than for the general population (Miniño et al., 2002). Alcohol use contributes to the three leading causes of death among African Americans between the ages of 12 and 20 years old. These causes of death are homicide, unintentional injuries (including car crashes), and suicide (National Center for Health Statistics Vital Statistics System, 2003).

It is commonly held that children move from having negative to positive alcohol expectancies due to alcohol advertising (DeBenedittis & Holman, 2010/2011). Connecting this social problem to hip-hop media, The Center on Alcohol Marketing and Youth (2003) released an executive summary that revealed widespread and pervasive overexposure of alcohol advertising to Black youth over non-Black youth. Nearly a decade after this research, Primack et al. (2011) conducted a qualitative content analysis of 793 songs featured in *Billboard Magazine* to identify songs that American adolescents were most exposed to from 2005 to 2007. Their findings revealed that one in five songs sampled from American popular music had explicit references to alcohol. More importantly, the scholars found that alcohol brand references were most prominent in Rap, Rhythm and Blues (R&B) and hip-hop music, suggesting that Blacks are heavily exposed to these potentially influential messages.

A decade and a half before Primack et al.'s (2011) study, Robert et al.'s (1999) study found that references to alcohol were more frequent in Rap (47% of songs) than other genres in its content analysis of 1,000 songs from 1996 to 1997. Also, the study determined that 48% of those rap songs had product placements or mentions of specific alcohol brand names. Rap music videos analyzed around the same time contained the highest percentage of depictions of alcohol use of any music genre appearing on MTV, BET, CMT, and VH-1 (DuRant et al., 1997). Alcohol consumption, in these media outlets, was portrayed as conveying elements of disinhibition, rebellion, and personal power among others.

Alcohol is often associated with complex and contradictory themes in hip-hop culture and surrounding Black communities. Alcohol consumption is promoted as paraphernalia of identity, pleasure, sensuality, and personal power among Rap artists. The fact that hip-hop artists market alcohol products and represent major Rap, R&B, and hip-hop labels further explains the prominence of branded alcohol references in these genres. Such synergistic marketing relationships between alcohol companies and the hip-hop industry create the power structures in hip-hop media that disproportionately target the Black youth community and encourage early alcohol consumption.

3   Hip-hop Music as a Major Form of Cultural Resistance
       for Black Youths

During the 1990s, Bakari Kitwana, editor of *The Source: The Magazine for Hip-hop Music, Culture, and Politics,* coined the term "hip-hop generation" to define the emerging population of Black youth (born between 1965 and 1984) who shared a value system that was at odds with the generations before them (Kitwana, 2002). Describing this same group of Black youth, Mark Anthony Neal used the term "post-soul" to describe the political, social, and cultural experiences of African Americans since the end of the Civil Rights and Black Power movements (Collins, 2006, p. 2). Neal (2002) argued that the "soul babies" of this period produced a "post-soul aesthetic whereby the hip-hop generation and the generational consciousness attached to it is now much broader than its origins in Black and Latino neighborhoods" (p. 3). Hip-hop culture has undoubtedly become a global phenomenon. However, Black youthremain its most visible ambassadors.

Contemporary hip-hop music, in many ways, is the postmodern incarnation of a traditional African American musical and rhetorical style (Rose, 1994). Rap and the larger context of hip-hop culture emerged among youth in the South Bronx neighborhoods of New York in the 1980s, replacing the fights and drugs associated with violent gang warfare in the 1970s (Herd, 1993, p. 740). For Black youth, hip-hop offered a populist arena for artistic expression, leadership, and later upward mobility in a society where they were being relegated in large numbers (Williams, 2017). Hip-hop music is regarded as a major form of cultural resistance and social protest for Black youth, who are increasingly alienated and disenfranchised in American cities suffering from police oppression and pervasive poverty (Durham, 2014). Black boys and men are often targets of increased police surveillance and attacks (Jackson, 2006). Instances of police oppression have become more prominent, resulting in the unjust victimization of Black youth.

The shift to new colorblind racism isolated and ghettoized Black youth within the American societal context (Sorrells, 2015). These social conditions have taken a cultural toll on Black youth. In *From Black Power to Hip-hop: Racism, Nationalism, and Feminism,* Patricia Hill Collins (2006) chronicled this shift from a color-conscious racism that depended on strict racial segregation to a seemingly colorblind racism. Colorblind racism promised equal opportunities, yet provided no lasting avenues for African-American advancement and, in turn, replicated racial hierarchy as effectively as the racial segregation of old (Collins, 2006, p. 3). Many Black youth no longer have access to the widespread public affirmations of racial pride that undergirded the Black Power movements of the 1960s and the generations before them (Kitwana, 2002).

Despite the soaring unemployment rates and low wages among African American families, the social worlds of Black youth are increasing penetrated by images of wealth and consumption that contradict their financially dismal realities. Within this oppressive setting, hip-hop music emerged as a form of social protest, allowing for the experience of subjugated knowledges using verbal, musical and iconic elements (Dyson, 1991). The strains of resistance, perpetuated by hip-hop music, are evidence of both social protest and affirmations of self-pride and personal dexterity (Rose, 2008). Hip-hop music offers strident student commentaries on ghettoized living conditions, racism, and police assaults (Kitwana, 2002). More contemporary hip-hop music contests the performer's uniqueness, creativity and sexual abilities. Based on these racial politics, hip-hop culture serves as a major vehicle for constructing and asserting political and personal identities for Black youth.

4 Hip-hop Media's Synergistic Relationship with the Alcohol Industry and Exploitation of Black Youth Communities

Pro-drinking images have been strategically placed within national youth media. These mediated images and messages often feature hip-hop artists to market alcohol content. The increased coverage of these artists signifies a much broader, problematic phenomenon in which fast food, athletic wear, cars, clothing and even food storage advertisements have used Rap music and hip-hop aesthetics to sell commodities (Stoute, 2012). The relatively high level of brand-name appearances related to alcohol in hip-hop music is indicative of strengthening ties between alcohol and music industries.

An early example of alcohol advertising in hip-hop media involved a marketing campaign launched by Saint Ides Malt Liquor in the early 1990s. This campaign included viral radio spots and television commercials that featured major Rap artists such as 2 Pac, Ice Cube, and Dr. Dre. The successful venture resulted in the establishment of major endorsement campaigns that provided music tour sponsorships and hosting events in clubs to featured artists (Herd, 2005). Through these practices, alcohol companies began to enter the music industry more formally. From 1995 to 2001, alcohol industry giant Seagram's acquired Universal and Polygram Records, merging the two labels to form the world's largest music conglomerate (Herd, 2005). Although Seagram's sold the label in 2001, the two companies maintained a synergistic marketing relationship, continuing to sponsor music tours and use individual artists in their promotions.

Alcohol marketing in hip-hop media continues to evolve with individual artists now establishing and promoting their own alcohol brands. These hip-hop artists include: Curtis '50 Cent' Jackson (Effen Vodka), Aubrey 'Virginia Black' Graham (Virginia Black Whiskey), Sean 'Jay-Z' Carter (Armadale Vodka), Jonathan 'Lil Jon' Smith (Little Jonathan Wineries), Christopher 'Ludacris' Bridges (Conjure Vodka), Onika 'Nicki Minaj' Maraj (Myx Fusion Moscato), Sean 'P. Diddy' Combs (Ciroc Vodka), Tip 'T.I.' Harris (Remy Martin Cognac), and Tremaine 'Trey Songz' Neverson (SX Liquors). It is important to emphasize that the aforementioned artists also represent major rap and hip-hop labels, serving as a potential explanation for the preponderance of branded alcohol references in these two genres. For example, in 2010, rapper Ludacris released a mixtape titled *Conjure: A Hustler's Spirit*. The mixtape featured numerous songs referencing his alcoholic beverage and even displayed a picture of the product on its cover. Similarly, female rapper Nicki Minaj has referenced her Myx Fusion Moscato brand in a number of songs including but not limited to: "Anaconda," "Bang Bang," "High School," "Only," and "The Night is Still Young."

Such product references and images are evidence of the relationships between the alcohol industry and Hip-hop. Black youth historically, have been protected from heavy consumption and problems due to cultural and religious factors (Harford & Lowman, 1989). Thus, the previously low drinking rates among young Blacks have made them a prime target for alcohol industry marketing. However, Black youth are now bombarded with alcohol advertisements at a time when they are experiencing unprecedented levels of deprivation, racism, and violence.

5   Hip-hop Pedagogy as an Entry Point to Alcohol-Specific
       Media Literacy

While prior research studies have placed heavy emphasis on the negative influences of hip-hop media on Black youth attitudes towards alcohol consumption, there has been a paucity of research exploring the pedagogical potential of hip-hop to decrease the prevalence of this societal problem through media literacy. Media literacy is integral to tackling the prominence of alcohol marketing in hip-hop media and its subsequent promotion of alcohol consumption to youth. Media literacy can be broadly defined as the ability to critically engage with media and cultural products, practices, or performances through the interpretive processes of deconstruction or contextualization, applied media production, advocacy, or political activism (Hobbs, 1998). In "Hip-hop Feminist Media Studies," Aisha Durham (2010) conceptualized media literacy "as required weaponry for the same minoritized youth who are assaulted with a barrage of controlling images and so-called negative media messages in popular hip-hop" (p. 120).

Recognizing the potential of media literacy to stage what Marc Lamont Hill (2009) described as critical pedagogies *of, about,* and *with* hip-hop, I draw from Durham's (2010) media literacy model of engaging hip-hop cultural products and performances. Durham's (2010) media literacy model identifies three entry points to offer classroom examples that reflect experiential, experimental hip-hop pedagogy: awareness, analysis, and advocacy (p. 124). While Durham (2010) developed this model from the stance of hip-hop feminist media studies, there are profound applications of her three entry points to this discussion of hip-hop media's promotion of alcohol consumption to Black youth. Incorporating her three-fold framework, I propose an approach to alcohol-specific media literacy that addresses the problematic marketing of alcohol to Black youth in hip-hop media. The aim of awareness is to understand the conversations that take place within hip-hop culture and the academic field of hip-hop studies and explore the aesthetic contributions and experiences of the groups that characterize the hip-hop generation (Durham, 2010). As an entry point in alcohol-specific media literacy centered on Black youth and hip-hop media, awareness asks students to explore the interrelationships between alcohol industries, hip-hop record labels, hip-hop artists, and the media. Moreover, it pushes students and teachers to investigate the political economy that undergirds the circulation of mainstream hip-hop music and its media. Through awareness, Black youth can connect the past with the present for the greater purpose of understanding the historical context in which hip-hop images were created and gained meaning.

The discourse on Black youth alcoholic consumption is more complex than the themes played out in contemporary hip-hop music. Hip-hop artists celebrate drinking and drunkenness as a part of a glorified lifestyle of partying and wild behavior. Alcohol use is associated with disinhibition and coupled with sensationalized imagery that serves as more than entertainment fodder for Black American youth. For this historically relegated population in the United States, alcohol use becomes a part of the limited repertoire for constructing social identities and dealing with social oppression. Students and teachers must acknowledge the unique standpoints of Black youth to investigate and raise critical points about their reactions to hip-hop's alcohol marketing during the awareness entry point. This intersectional analysis will expose the ways in which hip-hop has been commodified by the alcohol industry to usher harmful consumer products into youth communities.

As a second entry point in this media literacy approach, analyzing hip-hop media is useful for thinking critically about the ways in which messages and visual cultures are constructed and interpreted (Durham, 2010). The products of media culture require multidimensional, close, textual readings to analyze their various forms of discourse, ideological positions, narrative strategies, image constructions, and effects (Kellner, 2011, p. 11). Textual methods, such as discourse, semiotic, or rhetorical analyses, are beneficial in the analysis of media because they allow students to investigate the deeper social meanings in language and visual imagery (Faircough, 2003). Incorporating these strategies into an alcohol-specific media literacy model allows students to better understand how alcohol marketing and hip-hop media are constructed to target specific demographics.

By analyzing lyrical and visual content in hip-hop media, Black youth gain in-depth knowledge about the representations, stereotypes, and sexual scripts germane to hip-hop culture. Additionally, teaching youth early to recognize ruptures when viewing alcohol references in hip-hop media equips them with the analytical skills to understand that mainstream hip-hop media are not purposeless discourses, but rather produced under structural and cultural constraints. More importantly, their critical analyses of hip-hop media should aim to spark resistance efforts against hip-hop media and the alcohol industry's disproportionate marketing of alcoholic beverage products to Black youth in the United States.

Lastly, advocacy should push students to utilize their new knowledge acquired from hip-hop culture and classroom collaborative efforts to effect social change. Effective teachers must understand that all knowledge should be shared with students to provoke critical thought and social transformation. Recognizing this dynamic, an alcohol-specific, media literacy model centered on hip-hop media must have a community outreach component that educates a larger public of the alcohol-related health disparities facing Black youth and the role hip-hop media play in the social problem. While academic journals and research reports have been considered gatekeepers of knowledge in the academy, their intellectual reach is limited when compared to other forms of mass communication. In response to these shortcomings, hip-hop teachers must charge students to take ownership of their intellectual enlightenments and develop initiatives that provoke an open community exchange about the problematic marketing of alcohol in hip-hop music. These exchanges should aim to decrease the alarming rates of early-age, alcohol consumption among Black youth populations in the United States and investigate how hip-hop can be used to address the social problem it assisted in creating.

6   Conclusion

The absence of meaningful employment or opportunities for higher education has obscured the future for many Black American youth, creating a dependency on hip-hop media to paint the inaccurate, yet desired, portrait of upward mobility in an unjust, American caste system. Getting drunk, cruising in cars, and engaging in sexual acts have become major themes in hip-hop media and are performed by Black youth. The artistic form of hip-hop has been commodified by the alcohol industry to usher harmful consumer products into the Black youth community. hip-hop media, as a result, have co-opted into a system of domination that profits directly from marketing detrimental goods and images into an already marginalized population in American society.

Recognizing these factors, the historical context of hip-hop music and its media must be taken into account when critiquing the prominence of alcohol marketing targeted towards the Black American youth community. Hip-hop media are not just pointless discourses and images but encompass a deeper sociopolitical agenda that has undoubtedly migrated Black American youth. Under this prism, the commodification of hip-hop media by the alcohol industry is largely responsible for the migration of this historically marginalized population towards problematic consumption of alcohol. However, it is important to note that just as hip-hop has been commodified by alcohol industries to migrate Black youth towards alcohol consumption, teachers can also use hip-hop media as pedagogical tools to teach media literacy and decrease the alarming alcohol-related, health disparities among youth populations of all races in the United States.

References

Collins, P. H. (2006). *From Black power to hip-hop: Racism, nationalism, and feminism.* Philadelphia, PA: Temple University Press.

de Benedittis, P., & Holman, W. B. (2010/2011). *Challenging alcohol expectancies with media literacy as a prevention strategy.* Retrieved from http://medialiteracy.net/pdf/Challenging_Alcohol_Expectancies_With_Media_Literacy_as_a_Prevention_Strategy.pdf

DuRant, R. H., Rome, E. S., Rich, M., Allred, L., Emans, S. J., & Woods, E. R. (1997). Tobacco and alcohol use behaviors portrayed in music videos: A content analysis. *American Journal of Public Health, 87*(7), 1131–1135.

Durham, A. (2010). Hip-hop feminist media studies. *International Journal of Africana Studies, 16*(1), 117–140.

Durham, A. (2014). *Home with hip-hop feminism: Performances in communication and culture (Intersections in communications and culture).* New York, NY: Peterlang Publishing, Inc.

Dyson, M. (1991). Performance, protest, and prophesy in the culture of hip-hop. In J. Spencer (Ed.), *The emergency of Black and the emergence of rap* (p. 15). Durham, NC: Duke University Press.

Eaton, D. K., Kann, L., Kinchen, S., Shanklin, S., Ross, J., Hawkins, J., Harris, W. A., Lowry, R., McManus, T., Chyen, D., Lim, C., Brener, N. D., & Wechsler, H. (2012). Youth risk behavior surveillance: United States, 2011. *Morbidity and Mortality Weekly Report (MMWR) Surveill Summary, 61*(4), 1–162.

Fairclough, N. (2003). *Analyzing discourse: Textual analysis for social research.* Oxford: Routledge.

Grant, B. F., & Dawson, D. A. (1997). Age at onset of alcohol use and its association with DSM-IV alcohol abuse and dependence: Results from the national longitudinal alcohol epidemiologic survey. *Journal of Substance Abuse, 9*(1), 103–110.

Harford, T., & Lowman, C. (1989). *Alcohol use among Black and White teenagers.* In Research Monograph No. 18, Conference on the Epidemiology of Alcohol Use and Abuse Use among Ethnic Minority Groups, September 1985. Department of Health and Human Services, DHHS Publication, Rockville, MD.

Herd, D. (1989). *The epidemiology of drinking patterns and alcohol-related problems among U.S. Blacks.* In Research Monograph No. 18, Conference on the Epidemiology of Alcohol Use and Abuse Use among Ethnic Minority Groups, September 1985. Department of Health and Human Services, DHHS Publication. Rockville, MD.

Herd, D. (1993). Contesting culture: Alcohol-related identity movements in contemporary African-American communities. *Contemporary Drug Problems, 6*, 738–759.

Herd, D. (2005). Changes in the prevalence of alcohol use in rap song lyrics: 1979–1997. *Addiction, 100*, 1258–1269.

Hill, M. L. (2009). *Beats, rhymes and classroom life: Hip-hop pedagogy and the politics of identity.* New York, NY: Teachers College Press.

Hobbs, R. (1998). The seven great debates in the media literacy movement. *Journal of Communication, 48*(1), 16.

Jackson, R. L. (2006). *Scripting the Black masculine body: Identity, discourse, and racial politics in popular media.* Albany, NY: State University of New York Press.

Kellner, D. (2011). Cultural studies, multiculturalism, and media culture. In G. Dines & J. Humez (Eds.), *Gender, race, and class in media: A critical reader* (pp. 7–18). Thousand Oaks, CA: Sage Publications Inc.

Kitwana, B. (2002). *The hip-hop generation: Young Blacks and the crisis in African-American culture.* New York, NY: Basic Books.

Miniño, A. M., Arias, E., Kochanek, K. D., Murphy, S. L., & Smith, B. L. (2002). *Deaths: Final data for 2000* (National Vital Statistics Reports, Vol. 50, p. 15). Hyattsville, MD: National Center for Health Statistics.

National Center for Health Statistics Vital Statistics System. (2003). 10 leading causes of death, United States 2000, Black, both sexes. In *WISQARS Leading Causes of Death Reports, 1999–2000.* Retrieved from http://webapp.cdc.gov/sasweb/ncipc/leadcaus10.htm

Neal, M. A. (2002). *Soul babies: Black popular culture and the post-soul aesthetic.* New York, NY: Routledge.

Primack, B. A., Nuzzo, E., Rice, K. R., & Sargent, J. D. (2011). Alcohol brand appearance in U.S. popular music. *Addiction, 106*(9), 1–10.

Roberts, D. F., Henriksen, L., & Christenson, P. G. (1999). *Substance use in popular movies and music.* Washington, DC: Office of National Drug Control Policy.

Rose, T. (1994). *Black noise: Rap music and Black cultural resistance in contemporary American popular culture.* Middletown, CT: Wesleyan University Press.

Rose, T. (2008). *The hip-hop wars: What we talk about when we talk about hip-hop and why it matters.* New York, NY: Worth Publishers.

Sorrells, K. (2015). *Intercultural communication: Globalization and social justice.* Thousand Oaks, CA: Sage Publications Inc.

Stoute, S. (2012). *The tanning of America: How hip-hop created a culture that rewrote the rules of the new economy.* New York, NY: Gotham Books.

The Center on Alcohol Marketing and Youth. (2003). *Exposure of African-American youth to alcohol advertising.* Washington, DC: The Center on Alcohol Marketing and Youth.

Williams, M. L. (2017). White chicks with a gangsta' pitch: Gendered Whiteness in United States rap culture (1990–2017). *The Journal of Hip-Hop Studies, 4*(1), 50–93.

CHAPTER 15

Why the Ed in #HipHopEd Is Not Enough: How Social Workers & Educators Can Change the Game

Raphael Travis Jr. and Joshua Childs
@raptjr and @jaycee43public

1   Hip-hop, Social Work and Education

The mission of social work mission isto enhance human wellbeing and help meet the basic human needs of all people, with particular attention to the needs and empowerment of people who are vulnerable, oppressed, and living in poverty. A historic and defining feature of social work is the profession's focus on individual wellbeing in a social context and the wellbeing of society. Fundamental to social work is attention to the environmental forces that create, contribute to, and address problems in living (NASW, 1999).

As outlined by Whittlesey-Jerome (2013), social workers are also part of the growing trend among all helping professionals' "need to prove that the services they offer are necessary and valuable..." (p. 77). Social workers are placed/situated in schools to remove any barriers to the prioritized desirable outcome of academic success in youth, which is the primary purpose of education. Thus, social workers operate within an academic outcome frame, sometimes leaving the core mission of the profession as secondary.

Social workers play an integral role within schools. They "help students reach their potential within educational settings...by helping to mitigate obstacles that impede the ability of students to be successful behaviorally and academically" (Sweifach & LaPorte, 2013, p. 131). However, there is room for interpretation about the theories of change related to academic success, and how social workers facilitate [positive academic] change. The Empowerment-based Positive Youth Development model (EMPYD) suggests that specific components of positive youth development facilitate academic success (Travis & Leech, 2013). Social workers add flexibility to the boundaries between the traditional school day and available resources, capitalizing on opportunities for growth and well-being before, during and after the school day. Social workers' efforts extend far beyond the stereotypical counselor role of therapist.

Tyson (2003) and Baffour (Tyson & Baffour, 2004) were among the first to empirically link social work practice with hip-hop culture. They sought to simultaneously add to the research literature and effective practice strategies. Tyson built on the work of Delgado (2000) and others to outline how core principles of the social work profession, including the strengths perspective, cultural sensitivity, and social justice/empowerment, are consistent with hip-hop's cultural origins (Tyson, 2003, p. 2; Travis & Deepak, 2011). The value of integrating hip-hop was also connected to asset-building. These strategies can leverage young people's natural strengths, their resilience after successfully overcoming prior adversities, their unique creativity, and simply "their" interests (Tyson, 2003; Tyson & Baffour, 2004). Previous literature highlighted hip-hop culture with inpatient and outpatient therapeutic practice, education, and general youth work.

Fast forward to the present, and evidence continues to grow about both hip-hop's potential empowering influences (Lightstone, 2012; Tillie-Allen, 2005; Travis, 2012; Tyson et al., 2012), and potential risky influences (Travis & Bowman, 2012; Tyson et al., 2012). Educational literature has argued similarly at how hip-hop culture can be an effective tool across educational settings (Emdin, 2010; Hall, 2011; Petchauer, 2011b, 2012; Seidel, 2011). This chapter picks up on this earlier work and current research by asking, "How can we transcend existing silos of social work and education theory to bridge the professions, and simultaneously build upon the most empowering aspects of present day hip-hop culture?" We answer this question by examining the unique but overlapping landscapes of contemporary education and contemporary social work practice. We continue by discussing how high-stakes accountability has made educator and social worker interests converge more than ever. We conclude with how this leaves opportunity for greater synergy in theories of change through #HipHopEd, which has the potential to produce desirable outcomes for students' learning and well-being.

2   The Positive Development of Youth Inside and Outside of the Classroom

Empowerment-based Positive Youth Development (EMPYD) informs the hip-hop based Individual and Community Empowerment (ICE) framework (Travis & Deepak, 2011; Travis, 2012), and provides a blueprint for how to move hip-hop integrated strategies forward in a climate of high-stakes accountability within education. EMPYD builds on earlier ideas of positive youth development, by stating that *a sense of community*, and *active and engaged citizenship* are *necessary* components of healthy development, especially for youth of color (Travis & Leech, 2013). Second, the EMPYD model shows the ingredients of positive youth development interrelated in meaningful ways, resulting in small networks of variables within the model. For example, sense of community has many variable connections in the model and is a hub of network density. However, it also *augments* existing networks in the model (Travis & Leech, 2013).

3   EMPYD in the Classroom

One feature within the EMPYD model is the mastery network; comprising the constructs of *connection, confidence and competence* (Travis & Leech, 2013). This becomes *the community of mastery* network when within a system that reinforces mastery, such as a classroom or school. From a reform standpoint, the question becomes, how can we create environments within the classroom and every other education sponsored setting that invite "all" of young people's strengths and capacities to learn and contribute? How can we "uncover, inspire and cultivate" (Travis, 2010) the best of what our youth have to offer? How can we then build upon these talents, skills and interests in general, and in this case, specifically with attention to the richness of hip-hop culture?

4   Educators and Students: Coping within Climates of High-Stakes Accountability

Accountability in education emphasizes that teachers, administrators, schools, districts, and states show continuous improvement in student achievement (Fuhrman, 1999). Accountability rose to prominence during the standards based reform movements of the 1980s and early 1990s (Darling-Hammond, 2012; Hamilton, 2012). Since 2001, educators have been engrossed in a "new" accountability era under No Child Left Behind (NCLB), which focuses on high standards and rigorous standardized assessments. Today's teachers, school leaders, and district personnel are under increased pressure to show academic improvement in students. Current school accountability culture focuses on student outcomes and ways to prepare students to reach mandated benchmarks and assessment scores, thus leading to an array of federal, state, and district policies that focus on holding schools accountable for student achievement.

5   Educators up against the Wall: The Common Core

With increasing dissatisfaction with public education in the United States (Jones, 2012), federal and state policy makers have attempted various educational reforms to address low student test scores and unsatisfactory student achievement. One major reform has been the establishment of the Common Core State Standards (CCSS) (Mathis, 2010). According to McDonnell and Weatherford (2013), the CCSS "has the potential to become one of the most significant policy shifts in American education..." (p. 7). Forty-five of 50 states and the District of Columbia are in the midst of implementing the CCSS with the hope that it will positively influence teacher practices, promote higher expectations, and increase the level of rigor in schools (Kornhaber et al., 2014).

6   Students up against the Wall: Zero Tolerance

Students are expected to keep pace academically with these new standards while continuing to pass regular benchmarks of competency across grade levels. However, research indicates that there is widespread variability in the conditions and quality of students' learning environments (Kornhaber, 2014). Additionally, school climate is a strong indicator of the type(s) of disciplinary policies implemented to curb behavioral issues (Monahan et al., 2014).

To combat adolescent behavioral problems, schools began implementing zero-tolerance policies that removed students who compromised the learning environment, and since the implementation of zero-tolerance policies, suspensions and expulsions have increased (Fabelo et al., 2011; Monahan et al., 2014). As a result, researchers have argued that the school to prison pipeline has come into existence as a consequence of schools criminalizing minor disciplinary infractions (Fowler et al., 2010; Monahan et al., 2014).

7   Opportunity Knocks: #HipHopEd

One current educational innovation highlights both challenges and opportunities among efforts to improve student learning. #HipHopEd (through hip-hop integrated strategies), offers a unique way forward in improving learning outcomes for students. We discuss #HipHopEd in conjunction with the ICE model to help explain both promises and limitations of hip-hop integrated strategies. We conclude by identifying points of intersection for education and social work professionals.

8   #HipHopEd: Challenges and Opportunities

Hip-hop as a pedagogical tool can nurture the development of artistic skills in hip-hop's cultural elements, it can serve as a modality for helping students better understand and contextualize traditional educational content (Hall, 2011; Petchauer, 2011a), and it may be considered material to unpack and critically analyze for personal or community well-being (Bridges, 2012; Clay, 2006; Emdin, 2010; Petchauer, 2011a, 2011b; Prier & Beachum, 2008; Seidel, 2011; Tyson et al., 2012; Veltre & Hadley, 2012; Viega, 2012). Recent thinking about the priorities of hip-hop pedagogical orientations are: (a) a commitment to self-awareness, (b) a call to service, and (c) a resistance to social injustice (Bridges, 2012). Since these are not at first glance, distinctly academic outcomes, we must orient these priorities within a model that ensures that they are not mistakenly received by educators or administrators as distracting to academic outcomes. In fact, they are aligned with a broader understanding of how to promote youth development, and include student academic competencies and strategies to help improve their communities and schools. Empowerment-based hip-hop pedagogy can address educator challenges as well as student challenges.

Many hip-hop integrated strategies extend beyond the classroom and must also be accounted for in considering the best ways to help facilitate student growth. hip-hop integrated strategies can be educator driven, social work driven, and outside youth worker driven. We will discuss some of these other initiatives later in the chapter.

9   #HipHopEd: "What Are We Measuring?"

Current strategies for measuring hip-hop integrated interventions are still tenuous. Little consistency has been reached about what constitutes optimal outcomes within the context of hip-hop integrated education (or therapeutic) strategies. This is not to suggest that no meaningful outcomes have been identified, or that no useful information has come from prior research on hip-hop integrated strategies. Rather, little consensus exists for what should result from these strategies. Suggestions have been made by Travis and Maston (2014) that we should focus on measuring empowerment outcomes, operationalized as five dimensions of betterment outlined in the Individual and Community Empowerment Framework (ICE): *esteem, resilience, growth, community and change*. A range of measures were discussed specific to hip-hop interventions.

The ICE model is the hip-hop related manifestation of EMPYD principles (Travis, 2012). It also allows for the simultaneous presence of empowerment and risk. It explicitly accounts for environmental contexts as foundations for interventions. EMPYD provides an opportunity for measuring effectively hip-hop integrated strategies. Measurement may occur at one instance or over time for both understanding empowering and risky music engagement (i.e., ICE measure), or over time as a baseline and an outcome associated with the potential influence of the intervention (e.g., EMPYD measure). For example, the global question might be, "How well did this [hip-hop] experience facilitate more or less empowering engagement with music?"

10 Connecting Social Work and Education Using #HipHopEd as the Foundation

Social workers and educators can collaborate to help students feel at their best within the classroom, to learn and retain material efficiently, and develop a positive network of relationships among other students and adults (Travis & Leech, 2013). Current theorizing and research on positive youth development helps provide guidance about promising strategies social workers can use within school settings to improve students' success behaviorally and academically. As discussed earlier, current school dynamics such as disparities in quality of school resources, wide discretion in discipline resulting in disparities in suspensions and expulsions, low expectations, limited coordination among helping professionals, and insufficient attention to mental health issues pose unique threats to each element of the mastery network: connection, confidence, and competence, along with sense of community. These are systemic barriers to student success. We must build upon existing research and practice strategies to promote positive development and connect these strategies and professional roles to a framework specific to hip-hop culture and the functional values of music engagement.

11 #HipHopEd: Success Inside and Outside of the Classroom

What is #HipHopEd now? And more importantly, what can it be if we realize this new vision of individual and community empowerment that integrates education, all aspects of health, and an interdisciplinary team of professionals attuned to the nuances of the culture? At the present, it is a supportive social media scene for students, professionals, and artists across a wide range of professions and geographies that use hip-hop as strategy for meeting goals in their personal or professional lives. #HipHopEd has limitless potential. It shows glimpses of being a movement, as it cuts across all elements of culture, although often rhyme-centric, and it cuts across regional subcultures and styles. Each Tuesday night, the hashtag reinforces a sense of community and connectedness among its followers. It offers a safe space to share and exchange [tangible #HipHopEd information and resources], and to support the broader hip-hop culture and movement. Collaboration around #HipHopEd can build upon existing discipline's efforts, and help solidify an infrastructure for integrating hip-hop culture into education.

12   #HipHopEd: A Tipping Point

One could argue that we have reached the proverbial "Tipping Point" for comprehensive use of hip-hop integrated strategies. The artistic growth, and the availability of programs, initiatives and resources have created a fertile landscape for strategic use of hip-hop culture. Opportunities exist for major advancements in our educational and youth development infrastructure if we properly leverage our expertise, experience, and resources.

13   Where Do We Go from Here? Educators & Social Workers in the *New Hip-hop* Era

To begin, a significant myth about hip-hop culture must be eliminated, especially as it pertains to education. Many individuals rely on a false stereotype that hip-hop culture equates to poor, urban, and highest [education/violence] risk youth. Hip-hop integrated activities are too often relegated to the hardest to reach students. Public perception of hip-op is often associated with urban, low income, and low test scores. It reifies the false belief that hip-hop is only correlated with poor and low performing. However, what about rural, mixed income schools where test scores meet the national average – but where students do not feel engaged? What about suburban, high income schools with high test scores – but where students feel disconnected from the content or culturally disconnected? The present chapter however, is grounded in the assumption that #HipHopEd strategies have potential value for all students.

14   The Future Is Now

We can build upon existing knowledge and push #HipHopEd forward in a more authentic manner by: (1) developing common language and structure for discussing and measuring well-being pathways associated with hip-hop culture, (2) recognizing individual roles and points of synergy among social workers, teachers and other youth serving professionals, and (3) aligning with existing reform efforts so that hip-hop strategies are universal and not marginalized to strategies for students at highest risk of academic failure. Social workers have a unique opportunity to take leadership on many of these efforts because of their greater propensity to operate as insiders and outsiders within school settings. Social workers are often working outside of schools with other helping professionals and partner organizations, allowing greater opportunity for advocacy and system level discussions.

15   A Common Language and Structure for Meaningful Outcomes

It is essential that hip-hop integrated practices use common terminology, apply applicable concepts, and employ rigorous measurement principles. Consider how greater clarity about desired outcomes can help recognize points of agreement between #HipHopEd(ucators) and social workers. For example, the EMPYD model of healthy development complements the Common Core State Standards, addressing academic and behavioral issues, and it addresses individual and community-based outcomes (home-school; school-community; and broader systems change).

A working language and structure, and valid and reliable measurements of strategies seeking to promote healthy development and academic success are essential. The EMPYD scale is a valid and reliable measure for outcomes that captures the seven constructs of well-being within the model (i.e., connection, confidence, competence, caring, character, community, and engaged citizenship) (Travis & Childs, in progress). Adopting this language and structure for hip-hop integrated strategies places teachers and social workers in the roles of "connection anchors" and facilitators of opportunities to build a sense of community. Further, this requires greater understanding of both role differentiation and role hybridization. The complexity of youth needs within schools puts teachers in a situation where they can benefit from traditional social work knowledge and skills, while social workers can similarly benefit from knowledge of core teaching and educational system processes.

16   #HipHopEd 2020: Just Five Short Years from Now

Imagine that *Science Genius*-type strategies are the norm, where students are engaged from the first day of school, anxiously awaiting the next time to spit their newest creation. Imagine 4th period science fiercely attesting to the fact that their class is better than 7th period science. Imagine that No I.D., Kanye West, Mike WiLL Made-It, and all of their best producer protégés contract with the Department of Education to distribute beats to schools all over the nation. How might this influence overall well-being outcomes along with the standard academic objectives?

Imagine another grade level where a 2nd period social studies classroom focuses their lesson on the new Smart on Crime Initiative, criminal justice policy, zero tolerance and racial profiling – while integrating a range of current and past hip-hop songs on the subject, allowing the opportunity to create songs, but also mural art, mixtapes, and videos that integrate pictures, music and other material, allowing personalization with individual and community experiences with these topics. Imagine a stacked class unit, where math classes are joined with social studies classes to focus on the mathematics and statistical computations related to this unit. Imagine the school social worker involved both inside and outside of the classroom to help unpack and contextualize these issues and the artistic creations across the ICE dimensions of esteem, resilience, growth, community, and change – with simultaneous attention to risk (such as high risk coping strategies). Imagine projects that bridge school based knowledge, skills and attitudes gained with community-based initiatives around criminal justice. Imagine students revisiting their own school's zero-tolerance policies in partnership with educators and administrators to potentially advocate for changes. Imagine that this is not the exception, with all due respect to those schools that are blazing the trail in these areas. Rather, imagine this is the norm.

17   Conclusion

The possibilities are endless for #HipHopEd and the untapped potential of hip-hop and youth cultures. Educators and Social Workers are in ideal positions to help individuals and communities realize this potential. The first step is articulating exactly what we need to help our young people reach their potential. The second step is taking a stance for our roles in this process. The final step is aligning with and expanding upon existing systems of practice to better implement and measure our desired outcomes. Now we must move from #HipHopEd to #HipHopEd 2020 and make those images a reality; that is, move from popular with potential to effective and everywhere.

References

Bridges. (2012). Toward a pedagogy of hip-hop in urban teacher education. *The Journal of Negro Education, 80*(3), 325–338.

Clay, A. (2006). All I need is one mic: Mobilizing youth for social change in the post-civil rights era. *Social Justice, 33*(2), 105–121.

Darling-Hammond, L. (2010). *The flat world and education: How America's commitment to equity will determine our future.* New York, NY: Teachers College Press.

Delgado, M. (2000). *New arenas for community social work practice with urban youth.* New York, NY: Columbia University Press.

Emdin, C. (2010). *Urban science education for the hip-hop generation: Essential tools for the urban science educator and researcher.* Rotterdam, The Netherlands: Sense Publishers.

Fabelo, T., Thompson, M., Plotkin, M., Carmichael, D., Marchbanks III, M., & Booth, E. (2011). *Breaking schools' rules: A statewide study of how school discipline relates to students' success and juvenile justice involvement.* New York, NY: Council of State Governments Justice Center.

Fowler, D., Lightsey, R., Monger, J., & Aseltine, E. (2010). *Texas' school-to-prison pipeline: School expulsion, the path from lockout to dropout.* Austin, TX: Texas Appleseed.

Hall, M. (2011). *Education in a hip-hop nation our identity, politics & pedagogy* (Unpublished doctoral dissertation). University of Massachusetts, Amherst.

Hamilton, L. S., Stecher, B. M., & Yuan, K. (2012). Standards-based accountability in the United States: Lessons learned and future directions. *Education Inquiry, 3*(2), 149–170.

Jones, J. M. (2012, June 29). In U.S., private schools get top marks for education children. *Gallup Politics.* Retrieved April, 2014, from http://www.gallup.com/poll/156974/private-schools-top-marks-educating-children.aspx?utm_source=alert&utm_medium=email&utm_campaign=syndication&utm_content=morelink&utm_term=All

Kornhaber, M., Griffith, K., & Tyler, A. (2014). It's not education by zip code anymore – but what is it? Conceptions of equity under common core. *Education Policy Analysis Archives, 22*(4), 1–26.

Lightstone, A. (2012). The importance of hip-hop for music therapists. In S. Hadley & G. Yancey (Eds.), *Therapeutic uses of rap and hip-hop* (pp. 39–56). New York, NY: Routledge/Taylor & Francis Group.

Mathis, W. J. (2010). *The common core standards initiative: An effective reform tool?* Boulder, CO: Education and the Public Interest Center.

McDonnell, L. M., & Weatherford, M. S. (2013). Evidence use and the common core state standards movement: From problem definition to policy adoption. *American Journal of Education, 120*(1), 1–25.

Monahan, K., VanDerhei, S., Bechtold, J., & Cauffman, E. (2014). From the school yard to the squad car: School discipline, truancy, and arrest. *Journal of Youth and Adolescence, 43*(7), 1110–1122.

National Association of Social Workers. (1999). *Code of ethics of the national association of social workers.* Washington, DC: NASW Press.

Petchauer, E. (2011a). Knowing what's up and learning what you're not supposed to: Hip-hop collegians, higher education, and the limits of critical consciousness. *Journal of Black Studies, 42*(5), 768–790.

Petchauer, E. (2011b). I feel what he was doin': Responding to justice-oriented teaching through hip-hop aesthetics. *Urban Education, 46*(6), 1411–1432.

Petchauer, E. (2012). Sampling memories: Using hip-hop aesthetics to learn from urban schooling experiences. *Educational Studies, 48*, 137–155.

Prier, D., & Beachum, F. (2008). Conceptualizing a critical discourse around hip-hop culture and Black male youth in educational scholarship and research. *International Journal of Qualitative Studies in Education, 21*(5), 519–535.

Seidel, S. (2011). *Hip-hop genius: Remixing high school education.* Lanham, MD: The Rowman & Littlefield Publishing Group, Inc.

Sweifach, J., & LaPorte, H. (2013). Assessing use of the standards for social work practice with groups by school social workers: A national study. *Social Work with Groups, 36*(2–3), 130–144.

Tillie Allen, N. (2005). Exploring hip-hop therapy with high-risk youth. *Praxis, 5*, 30–36.

Travis, R. (2010). What they think: Attributions made by youth workers about youth circumstances and the implications for service-delivery in out-of-school time programs. *Child Youth Care Forum, 39*(6), 443–464.

Travis, R. (2012). Rap music and the empowerment of today's youth: Evidence in everyday music listening, music therapy, and commercial rap music. *Child and Adolescent Social Work Journal, 30*(2), 139–167.

Travis, R., & Bowman, S. (2012). Ethnic identity, self-esteem, depression and variability in rap music's influence on empowering and risky behaviors. *Journal of Youth Studies, 15*(4), 455–478.

Travis, R., & Childs, J. (in progress). *Theoretical and empirical consistency of a measure of empowerment-based positive youth development with a multi-racial sample.*

Travis, R., & Deepak, A. (2011). Empowerment in context: lessons from hip-hop culture for social work practice. *Journal of Ethnic & Cultural Diversity in Social Work, 20*, 203–222.

Travis, R., & Leech, T. (2013). Empowerment-based positive youth development: A new understanding of healthy development for African American youth. *Journal of Research on Adolescence, 24*(1), 93–116.

Travis, R., & Maston, A. (2014). Hip-hop and pedagogy, more than meets the eye: What do we expect, what will we measure? In B. Porfilio, D. Roychoudhury, & L. Gardner (Eds.), *See you at the crossroads: Hip-hop scholarship at the intersections: Dialectical harmony, ethics, aesthetics, and panoply of voices.* Rotterdam, The Netherlands: Sense Publisher.

Tyson, E. (2003). Rap music in social work practice with African American and Latino youth: A conceptual model with practical applications. *Journal of Human Behavior in the Social Environment, 8*(4), 1–21.

Tyson, E., & Baffour, T. (2004). Arts-based strengths: A solution-focused intervention with adolescents in an acute-care psychiatric setting. *The Arts in Psychotherapy, 31,* 213–227.

Tyson, E., Detchkov, K., Eastwood, E., Carver, A., & Sehr, A. (2012). Therapeutic uses of rap and hip-hop. In S. Hadley & G. Yancey (Eds.), *Therapeutic uses of rap and hip-hop* (pp. 99–114). New York, NY: Routledge/Taylor & Francis Group.

Veltre, V., & Hadley, S. (2012). It's bigger than hip-hop: A hip-hop feminist approach to music therapy with adolescent females. In S. Hadley & G. Yancy (Eds.), *Therapeutic uses of rap and hip-hop* (pp. 79–98). New York, NY: Routledge/Taylor & Francis Group.

Viega, M. (2012). The hero's journey hip-hop and its applications in music therapy. In S. Hadley & G. Yancy (Eds.), *Therapeutic uses of rap and hip-hop* (pp. 57–78). New York, NY: Routledge/Taylor & Francis Group.

Whittlesey-Jerome, W. (2013). Results of the 2010 statewide New Mexico school social work survey: Implications for evaluating the effectiveness of school social work. *School Social Work Journal, 37*(2), 76–87.

CHAPTER 16

Aligning Community Defined Practice with Evidence Based Group Counseling: The Hip-hop Cypher as Group Counseling

Ian P. Levy
@Ianplevy

1 Introduction

Well you trippin if you think I'm gonna sit on this couch/
And tell this shrink what my deeply rooted problems about/
The words out my mouth like acts of vengeance/
From the blackest dungeons in a mass abundance/
We move together like shadows and figures/
We strike when we like, with a mind like the Gravediggaz/
Painted pictures and still photography/
Movin images, reverse psychology/
      PREVAIL

In contemporary America, there are segments of the population that are consistently underserved by social work professionals. These populations occupy neighborhoods in urban America that are not only lacking in terms of access to, and quality of mental health services, but are often stigmatized for seeking the sparse ones that do exist. They are from racial/ethnic and socioeconomic backgrounds where their everyday realities require avenues for voice, healing, and reflection. However, because of the disparities in social work and counseling, they have responded to being locked out of traditional spaces designed to help them to heal by creating their own. I open this chapter with rapper Prevail's words, highlighting feelings towards traditional health professionals, but also what happens within community-based, non-traditional healing spaces. Prevail shines a light on significant and under-focused upon dimensions of the mental health care system in America by speaking to the negative stance on traditional mental health services held by those marginalized from them. When he states that *"you trippin if you think I'm gonna sit on this couch, and tell this shrink what my deeply rooted problems about"* Prevail is discussing a stigma that he, and others who identify as hip-hop, tend to have towards counseling services/therapy. This stigma is known to have various roots, and has often left young people of color with the responsibility of developing community defined approaches for healing (Levy, 2014). For Prevail, not finding the "shrink's couch" to be a comfortable space for addressing his mental health needs moves him towards hip-hop. Hip-hop lyrics become a form of therapy as they provide a path towards healing – *"the words out my mouth like acts of vengeance."* Hip-hop culture becomes a form of group therapy as he and his crew *"move together like shadows and figures."* To understand where the stigma that is held regarding traditional mental health spaces comes from, come from, we must delve deeply into the context(s) where this stigma is born, and to address the needs of populations who are looking for productive options to address their mental health needs, we must confronted and inform the field of mental health with new models that interrogate the ways that marginalized populations have dealt with mental health stressors outside of traditional structures.

Prevail's frustration reflects the outcomes of current literature in health education which suggests that young people from urban environments are approximately one-third to one-half less likely to be provided with mental health care than White youth (Holm-Hansen, 2006). Holm-Hansen (2006) further argues that even when care is provided to these young people, disparities are evident in the quality and completion of those services. This is likely due to highly westernized approaches to counseling and therapy deployed in America, which have been consistently addressed by researchers as both inadequate and potentially harmful to individuals of diverse ethnic and racial backgrounds (Griner & Smith, 2006). The lack of culturally responsive mental health outlets for individuals of color is itself reflective of the a-cultural nature of mental health practice writ large and indicative of a robust set of disparities that breed feelings of isolation, distaste, and lack of appreciation for mental health services among urban youth of color (Griner & Smith, 2006; Chandra & Minkovitz, 2007).

2 Stress, Distrust and Their Repercussions

The same youth who are subject to mental health disparities live in environments that place them under higher levels of emotional distress (Stockdale et al., 2007). Existing research has made it abundantly clear that the neighborhood and community have a direct effect on an individual's mental health, and that urban neighborhoods are at a disadvantage when it comes to social and economic resources, leading to higher levels of physical and social disorders (Sampson et al., 1997). Because stressors created by the environment often manifest themselves in lower levels of trust and higher levels of social isolation (Ross et al., 2000), it is important to consider that the absence of resources becomes coupled with a mistrust of traditional mental health systems and increases in the likelihood of depression, anxiety, substance abuse, and psychological distress (Latkin & Curry 2003; Boardman et al., 2001; Ross, 2000; Aneshensel & Sucoff, 1996).

The distrust birthed from an absence of resources has informed research on perceptions of gender norms among young men of color. These populations are willing to express emotion and often feel like they need to uphold a hard exterior. Research indicates that young men of color who experience environmental stressors, cultivate a level of inexpressiveness (Polce-Lynch, Myers, Kilmartin, Forssmann-Falck, & Kliewer, 1998; Polce-Lynch, Myers, Kliewer, & Kilmartin, 2001) that indicates a distrust of people or systems around them. Expressing vulnerability is seen as a weakness and this phenomenon further stigmatizes mental health systems/services. In fact, research indicates that inexpressiveness and the absence of vulnerability is supported within communities where mental health systems are broken and do not reflect what is needed by the community (Balswick, 1988; Brooks, 1998; Moore & Haverkamp, 1989; Pollack & Levant, 1998; Scher, 1981).

3   Therapeutic Factors in Group Counseling

Traditionally, scholars have explored the use of a group therapy model for addressing the mental health stressors and trauma youth encounter (Kohn et al., 2002; Carter et al., 2003). Researchers have found that within group therapy, individuals can engage in conversations based on their lived experiences, pinpoint emotional experiences they have in common, and troubleshoot solutions (Yalom & Leszcz, 2005). The facilitation of emotion based conversations in group therapy allows group members to relate to each other and the content in a much different way than they traditionally do. Yalom (2008) explains eleven primary therapeutic factors that must be present for the group process to occur. These factors are: *instillation of hope, universality, imparting information, altruism, the corrective recapitulation of the primary family group, development of socializing techniques, imitative behavior, interpersonal learning, group cohesiveness, catharsis, and existential factors* (Yalom, 2008). All of these factors are said to be the foundation for effective therapy.

Instillation of hope is described as members accepting that therapy will be helpful for them based on the fact that they see other members have improved (Yalom, 2008). Universality is best described as the group member's realization that they are among people who share their feelings of discomfort. When universality is present within a group, members are more apt to share their experiences so they can, feel supported and validated by others, and potentially gain insight regarding coping strategies. A healthy therapeutic environment emerges when members of the group feel they are understood because other members have similar feelings and thoughts, they realize they are not alone (Yalom, 2008).

The imparting of information within group counseling happens in two ways; didactic instruction and direct advice (Yalom, 2008). Didactic instruction is psychoeducation in which group members learn more about how their particular problem or illness affects them. On the other hand, direct advice usually functions as strategies or recommendations on how to cope (Yalom, 2008).

Altruism occurs when a member raises his or her self-esteem after/ by helping someone. Knowing that their personal struggles can be worth something to others creates a great boost of self-confidence for these members (Yalom, 2008). Yalom (2008) mentions that clients who have difficult family experiences benefit from group therapy because the experience because the close environment where members self-disclose and emote resembles a family. If a group member is able to have healthy relationships with various individuals in their group, this can act as a correction to a lot of unsuccessful or negative experiences they had, or continue to have, within their family (Yalom, 2008).

Socializing techniques are another positive aspect to the group environment. The atmosphere can be conducive to working through conflict and learning to effectively self-disclose with fellow members. Over time this type of environment can foster a change in communication for group members from dysfunctional, to more effective. It is important for individuals to realize that healthy communication implies that conflict will arise, but it can be worked through. A group experience can help members become more comfortable expressing themselves, and in turn build healthier relationships (Yalom, 2008). Additionally, this can lead members to develop imitative behavior. Since this atmosphere has been created, newer members are given the chance to watch others partake in self-exploration, work through it, and make significant personal developments. Catharsis, or strong feelings being released about past experiences, can allow other members a chance to feel they can do the same. These existential factors allow members the chance to move forward with their lives in a more productive and self-aware fashion (Yalom, 2008). All in all, each aforementioned group factor provides members, in some fashion, with a sense of trust, belongingness, and togetherness. These feelings explain another crucial therapeutic factor called cohesiveness (Yalom, 2008).

The last three factors, interpersonal learning – input, interpersonal learning – output, and self-understanding, complement each other and foster powerful group interaction. By being open about their experiences to the rest of the group (input), members provide an opportunity for others to provide them with feedback. This feedback allows them to gain valuable personal insight regarding how they impact others (Yalom, 2008). This type of honest exploration cannot happen if the environment is not conducive for it. All members work together to create an open environment for individuals to try own new roles and learn more about themselves interpersonally. This type of learning is called interpersonal learning – output (Yalom, 2008). Acceptance of constructive feedback is necessary for members to gain insight into their own psychological motivation, which dictates their emotional and behavioral reactions. Realizations made regarding one's psychological motivation is referred to as self-understanding (Yalom, 2008).

I take the position that groups in social work practice must be used with communities who traditionally are exposed to mental health care disparities. The use of groups in social work practice has a vast array of evidence to support its effectiveness as a therapeutic medium. It is unfortunate however that certain populations are unable to access said services, particularly those populations who experience higher levels of stress. Consequently, I suggest it is necessary for social work professionals to begin identifying community defined practices they've created as a means for their own healing as models for group therapy. I argue that by coupling existing community defined practices with group counseling methodologies we can accentuate the power and potential of group social work practices, particularly for those who face disparities that bar them from acquisition of traditional mental health services.

4   Cypher as Community Defined Practice

As researchers we hold a vested interest in identifying practices that various communities deploy in order to create avenues for healing amidst mental health care disparities. These practices are valuable for the community itself because they emerge directly from cultural practices. In a recent excursion in the South Bronx I discovered a handful of black and brown youth engaging in a hip-hop cypher on a street corner. Hip-hop cyphers are highly codified yet unstructured practices where youth who identify with hip-hop culture exchange information in the form of raps or dance. Interestingly enough, these same youth participating in the hip-hop cypher represent a population that is known to face various barriers in regards to their access to adequate mental health care, and subsequently are often left with unaddressed forms of emotional distress and trauma. However, within this space, these youth appeared to be working through those unaddressed thoughts and feelings. In observing the interactions of these youth within the cypher, it became apparent that the cypher itself acted as a community generated form of group therapy. The cypher, which emerges from cultural practices of urban youth, is a modern rendition of African drum circles. African music as a social and cultural practice was designed for collective community building and emotional release (Anku, 2000). As much as drum circles are used within African culture as places for socialization, they also create space for individuals to build community and work through issues that arise (Anku, 2000). Furthering this idea, Snow and D'Amico (2010) found that the integration of West African drum circles in their urban high school counseling program resulted in various therapeutic benefits for students. That is to say that the therapeutic factors group theorists define as necessary for effective therapy, existed within the natural structure of the hip-hop cypher, which originated from traditional African drum circles.

Underlying the inherent therapeutic processes that occur within hip-hop cyphers is a specific structure and set of unspoken rules that govern group interactions. As the participants share with each other, the following rules appeared to be in place: (1) everyone had a chance to share, (2) all voices had equal value, (3) praise was awarded to individuals when they did share, and (4) equal support was provided to participants when in need. In this cypher, and in others, these norms converge to create a sense of comfort and belonging for group members, what Yalom and Leszcz (2005) would define as cohesiveness. It is then through this cohesiveness that various therapeutic factors are able to exist within the hip-hop cypher.

In a successful group counseling setting, therapists hope for a presence of altruism. Yalom and Leszcz (2005) speak specifically about the importance of support amongst group members. Within our observations of the cypher, there were multiple moments where the participants rallied behind individuals while they rapped. For example, the group may decide to slow their beat down to create easier rhythms for more timid and novice rappers to share their lyrics over, or they may chant statements like "oohh!!", or "Go in, go in, go in!!" to encourage more rhyming, which in turn provides a welcoming space for individuals to express emotional content.

When newcomers enter the cypher, they may be hesitant to share their stories, or may lack the necessary vocabulary and/or social skills to succinctly speak to how they feel. However, the structure of the hip-hop cypher sets the stage for group members to develop what Yalom (2008) calls Socialization Techniques. Within the hip-hop cypher, participants may engage in rhyming activities specifically designed for the betterment of the rhyming of all participants. For instance, participants may take turns reciting four bars each (in hip-hop cyphers bars are referred to as measures), passing the floor to another group member after they are done. As opposed to asking a newcomer to recite 16 bars, this gives newer group members a chance to slowly cultivate a new way of talking about their thoughts and feelings in cypher based conversation.

Cyphers also lend themselves to catharsis and interpersonal learning for group members. Inside of hip-hop cyphers it is commonplace for folks to share their personal narratives through rhyme. This is likely because hip-hop culture was birthed out of the need to push back against forms of oppression, and is rooted in storytelling (Chang, 2007). Therefore, when cyphers come together and participants share their individual narratives, the group is afforded the chance to find out more information about their group members, and subsequently themselves. This allows cyphers to produce an atmosphere for interpersonal learning and catharsis to occur. It is also important to mention that by engaging emotional expression through the socially and culturally appropriate medium of rhyming, male participants in particular are countering issues with inexpression. This is important because one of the main deterrents for the acquisition of mental health services for men of color are socialized gender norms which suggest to men that if they are emotional they are not as masculine (Polce-Lynch, Myers, Kilmartin, Forssmann-Falck, & Kliewer, 1998; Polce-Lynch, Myers, Kliewer, & Kilmartin, 2001). The hip-hop cypher counters that fear of being/seeming vulnerable with a sense of cultural credibility, allowing cypher participants the chance to release difficult emotional experiences that they otherwise could not, for fear of being judged.

When newcomers enter the cypher they see others sharing stories, and showcasing ability to adequately explain their thoughts and feelings through rhyme. As they begin to participate they receive support based on both the norms of engagement which exist within the cypher, and through the use of rhyme activities designed to help them better their socialization techniques. By observing more seasoned participants sharing their narratives, within the cypher, using emotionally descriptive and succinct language, they engage in what Yalom and Leszcz (2005) dubbed imitative behavior.

As members learn more about one another through rhyme and participating in the cypher, supporting each other in times of need, and through developing better socialization techniques, the group naturally becomes more cohesive. Yalom and Leszcz (1995) define cohesiveness as "the condition of members feeling warmth and comfort in the group, feeling they belong, valuing the group and feeling, in turn, that they are valued and unconditionally accepted and supported by the other members" (p. 48).

Through engaging in the hip-hop cypher, participants have been afforded the opportunity of being part of a group that naturally contains various therapeutic factors deemed necessary for an effective therapeutic experience.

The hip-hop cypher is an example of a practice deployed by the community itself to heal, amidst mental health care disparities. Without anywhere else to turn, this particular community tapped into their African roots and built a space to process emotions. However, emotional issues still go unresolved in these communities, and gaps in the acquisition of mental health services still exist. The work this community has done to create avenues for healing through the hip-hop cypher is laudable, but they are in need of help to further their healing.

5   Introducing Community Defined Practice to Accentuate Evidence Based Theory

I argue that in order to allow marginalized communities access to the therapeutic power and potential of groups in social work practice, we must consider the cultural practices for healing within said communities. In the particular case of black and brown youth in urban communities, the hip-hop cypher has been developed as a modernized form of the African cultural drum circle to be used to combat difficult emotional issues. While the hip-hop cypher has provided a valuable outlet for urban communities in times of need, urban communities of color are still exposed to a multitude of mental health disparities (Holm-Hansen, 2006). If social workers wish to utilize groups as a therapeutic intervention with urban communities, they must consider how to integrate the hip-hop cypher into their traditional group social work practice. In doing so, social workers can help demystify the stigma held towards mental health care services by creating a culturally acceptable space for urban youth to emote (pushing back against male gender norms which promote inexpressiveness and refusal of mental health services) and a culturally responsive form of therapy (which the lack thereof has traditionally led to ineffective therapy for communities of color). By allowing the cypher to enter a traditional counseling space, the social worker positions themselves to not only accentuate their own practice, but may also accentuate the cypher. Participants who have found the cypher to be a place where they have grown can be positioned to reach even higher levels of healing, due to the conscious effort of the facilitator to guide the cypher towards its maximum therapeutic potential.

In order to assist social workers with the integration of the hip-hop cypher into their group practice, we provide the following tangible tools. Corey (2009) speaks to the power of including a group "check-in" at the start of each group. This is a space for the group, and the facilitator, to access where everyone in the group is emotionally at the start of the session. This can dictate the trajectory of the session, as it helps the group pinpoint the emotional states of each group member (Corey, 2009). Often times in a check-in, a group member may bring up an emotion or a recent experience that resonates with the group, causing that to become the theme for that given session (Corey, 2009).

To create a more culturally sensitive "check-in" we recommend group counselors play a hip-hop instrumental beat, and have group members check-in through rhyme. This can either be done through freestyle (where members recite unwritten rhymes off the top of their head), or can be done with written rhymes. If group counselors make an effort to have group members create rhymes in a journal based on the emotions they experience between sessions, then they can use those rhymes to check-in at the start of the session. Both the freestyle and written rhyme option allow the facilitator to pick up on the state of mind group members are in at the start of the session. For example, one group member shares a rhyme about an argument they had with a parent, and if the rest of the group responds emphatically, this may be a good opportunity for the social worker to hone in on family drama as the theme for that session. In this event the facilitator could engage in a therapeutic dialogue about family issues the group is facing with the purpose of then having the group construct rhymes specifically about family drama. The facilitator could place an instrumental hip-hop beat on and have each member write about their family. When complete the group can return to the cypher and share out their verses.

Another example is the use of a Gestalt Therapy intervention called the empty chair technique, which has been documented by researchers as a medium through which clients show decreases in stress and anger (Beutler et al., 1986). Wagner-Moore (2004) explains the empty chair technique as a role-playing exercise in which a client sits facing an empty chair. In that empty chair they imagine a person whom they have some conflict with (an example may include being angry at your boss). The participant sitting in the chair then begins to pretend they are in conversation with their boss, engaging in role-play. They may be asked mid conversation to switch seats, therefore taking on the position their boss in the conversation (Wagner-Moore, 2004). This method is designed to have a client sort through negative feelings they have based on a relationship in their life (Wagner-Moore, 2004).

In a hip-hop cypher a facilitator can use this approach by placing two chairs inside the circle. With a beat playing over the speakers the facilitator can ask a group member to take a seat in one chair, and recite rhymes towards the empty chair. If the theme is family issues, the group social worker could ask the group to, "imagine a family member you are in conflict with and pretend they are sitting in the chair across from you," if more guidance is necessary they could add a statement such as, "while the beat is playing I want you to recite a rhyme where you play out a conversation with that family member, expressing your true feelings." The facilitator may then ask the participant to switch seats to rhyme from the family member's point of view, or could choose to have another group member sit in the chair and rhyme. This process could be utilized for the same reasons as the empty chair technique, to sort through negative emotions regarding a relationship in one's life. The empty chair technique mimics a common practice within the hip-hop cypher called "the battle," or a "head-to-head," where two participants square off against one another. This functionality in the cypher, if introduced by the facilitator in a careful way, can function as a culturally responsive version the empty chair technique.

We recommend social workers use these two tangible methods for the integration of the hip-hop cypher into their group counseling practice. By integrating "the battle" or the "head-to-head" into their practice, group counselors can pull from the empirically validated empty chair technique as a platform for role-play. In addition, social workers can work to utilize the hip-hop cypher during check-in to and get a feel for the emotions members are bringing into the room with them. This can allow for the identification of emotional themes the group can discuss openly with each other. Through focusing on these two interventions, social workers will accentuate the power of group counseling practice by allowing it to be more accessible to urban communities.

6 Conclusion

I highlight the power and potential of using groups in social work practice. However, we also lament the fact that certain communities are unable to access said services due to numerous mental health care disparities. Consequently, I suggest that when communities are faced with mental health care inequalities, they work collectively to create their own outlets for healing which are often rooted in the cultural practices of the given community. By investigating these different mediums through which communities in need create their own methods of healing, social work professionals can work to find ways to include a given communities cultural healing practices inside their own group counseling practice. It is often the case that these community defined practices allow for levels of catharsis, but can be built upon further if they are allowed to enter more traditionally defined therapeutic environments.

Specifically, we focus on the hip-hop cypher as an example of a community defined practice for healing which, if integrated with evidence based group counseling theory, holds promise in countering the mental health disparities that plague black and brown communities. I found that within the hip-hop cypher there was an inherent presence of therapeutic group factors necessary for effective therapy. As a result we concluded the hip-hop cypher may be combined with evidence based group counseling interventions, and presented tangible solutions for social works to utilize to accentuate their practice. While the ideas presented have value within group counseling practice, more research is necessary to empirically justify their therapeutic effectiveness.

References

Anku, W. (2000). Circles and time: A theory of structural organization of rhythm in African music. *Music Theory Online, 6*(1).

Author. (2010). Affiliation and alienation: Hip-hop, rap, and urban science education. *Journal of Curriculum Studies, 42*(1), 1–25.

Author. (2014). Hip-hop emotional exploration in men. *Journal of Poetry Therapy, 27*(4), 217–223.

Chang, J. (2007). *Can't stop won't stop: A history of the hip-hop generation.* New York, NY: Macmillan.

Corey, G. (2009). *Theory and practice of counseling and psychotherapy* (8th ed.). Belmont, CA: Brooks/Cole.

Griner, D., & Smith, T. B. (2006). Culturally adapted mental health intervention: A meta-analytic review. *Psychotherapy: Theory, Research, Practice, Training, 43*(4), 531–548. doi.org/10.1037/0033-3204.43.4.531

O'Malley, L., & Ryan, A. (2006). Pedagogy and relationship marketing: Opportunities for frame restructuring using African drumming. *Journal of Marketing Management, 22*(1–2), 195–214.

Petchauer, E. (2009). Framing and reviewing hip-hop educational research. *Review of educational research, 79*(2), 946–978.

Snow, S., & D'Amico, M. (2010). The drum circle project: A qualitative study with at-risk youth in a school setting. *Canadian Journal of Music Therapy, 16*(1), 12–39.

Tuckman, B. (1965). Developmental sequences in small groups. *Psychological bulletin, 63*, 384–399.

Wagner-Moore, L. E. (2004). Gestalt therapy: Past, present, theory, and research. *Psychotherapy: Theory, Research, Practice, Training, 41*(2), 180.

Yalom, I. D. (2008). *The theory and practice of group psychotherapy* (5th ed.). New York, NY: Basic Books.

Yalom, I. D., & Leszcz, M. (1995). *The theory and practice of group therapy.* Chicago, IL: Chicago University Press.

Yalom, I. D., & Leszcz, M. (2005). *Theory and practice of group psychotherapy.* New York, NY: Basic books.

Printed in the United States
By Bookmasters